Who Was a Daring Pioneer of the Skies?

AMELIA EARHART

T0008751

For the truth-seekers—MG

For my teachers, who kept their sights, and
those of their students, on the horizon—ACE

PENGUIN WORKSHOP
An imprint of Penguin Random House LLC, New York

First published in the United States of America by Penguin Workshop,
an imprint of Penguin Random House LLC, New York, 2022

Visit us online at penguinrandomhouse.com.

Library of Congress Cataloging-in-Publication Data is available.

Manufactured in China

ISBN 9780593224656 (pbk)
ISBN 9780593224663 (hc)

10 9 8 7 6 5 4 3 HH
10 9 8 7 6 5 4 3 2 1 LEG

Lettering by Comicraft
Design by Jay Emmanuel

This is a work of nonfiction. All of the events that unfold in the narrative
are rooted in historical fact. Some dialogue and characters have been fictionalized
in order to illustrate or teach a historical point.

The publisher does not have any control over and does not assume
any responsibility for author or third-party websites or their content.

For more information about your favorite historical figures, places, and events,
please visit whohq.com.

A WHO HQ GRAPHIC NOVEL

Who Was a Daring Pioneer of the Skies?

AMELIA EARHART

by Melanie Gillman
illustrated by A.C. Esguerra

Penguin Workshop

Introduction

Amelia Earhart was born on July 24, 1897, into a well-to-do family in the small town of Atchison, Kansas. From an early age, she loved adventure: Her hobbies included climbing trees, hunting, collecting insects, and building makeshift roller coasters on the roof of her family's toolshed.

While Amelia was growing up, the field of flying airplanes (known as aviation) was also beginning to take off. Early aviation pioneers in both Europe and the United States experimented with small aircraft called gliders throughout the 1890s. In 1903, the Wright brothers pulled off the first successful powered airplane flight—traveling just 120 feet over the sand dunes of Kitty Hawk, North Carolina. By 1915, airplanes were sophisticated enough that entire battles could be fought in the air during World War I.

After the war, many of those World War I military aviators became stunt pilots, performing dives and barrel rolls at fairs all over the United States. In 1920, one such former World War I pilot let Amelia ride in his plane as a passenger for ten minutes—and she was immediately hooked. She began saving up money for flying lessons.

Once she began flying, it didn't take long for Amelia to start setting records. By 1922, she held the unofficial record for the highest altitude reached by a woman pilot. In 1928, she became the first woman to fly across the Atlantic as a passenger—and in 1932, she became the first woman to fly across the Atlantic as a solo pilot. From then on, she was a household name.

Amelia accomplished all this even though, at the time, many people believed that women should not be pilots at all! Because aviation was such a difficult and dangerous occupation, people thought only men could do it. Amelia made it her life's work to oppose this idea and to prove that this way of thinking was sexist and wrong.

As Amelia's fame grew, her aviation career was managed with the help of her husband, G. P. Putnam. G. P. was a savvy businessman. He knew how to make his wife an aviation celebrity and then how to turn that fame into profit. He kept Amelia busy writing books, delivering lectures, and endorsing products, many of which were not related to aviation at all—such as watches, chewing gum, tomato juice, and cigarettes.

In 1937, Amelia was in the middle of cooking up plans for a new record-setting flight—one where she would circle the entire globe at the equator. First, she would need a *lot* of money to complete the trip. If she was successful, though, both she and G. P. knew they could make a fortune off her increased fame. Just as importantly to Amelia—if she made it all the way around the globe, she would help show the whole world that women were capable of great feats in aviation. And Amelia never backed down from a challenge.

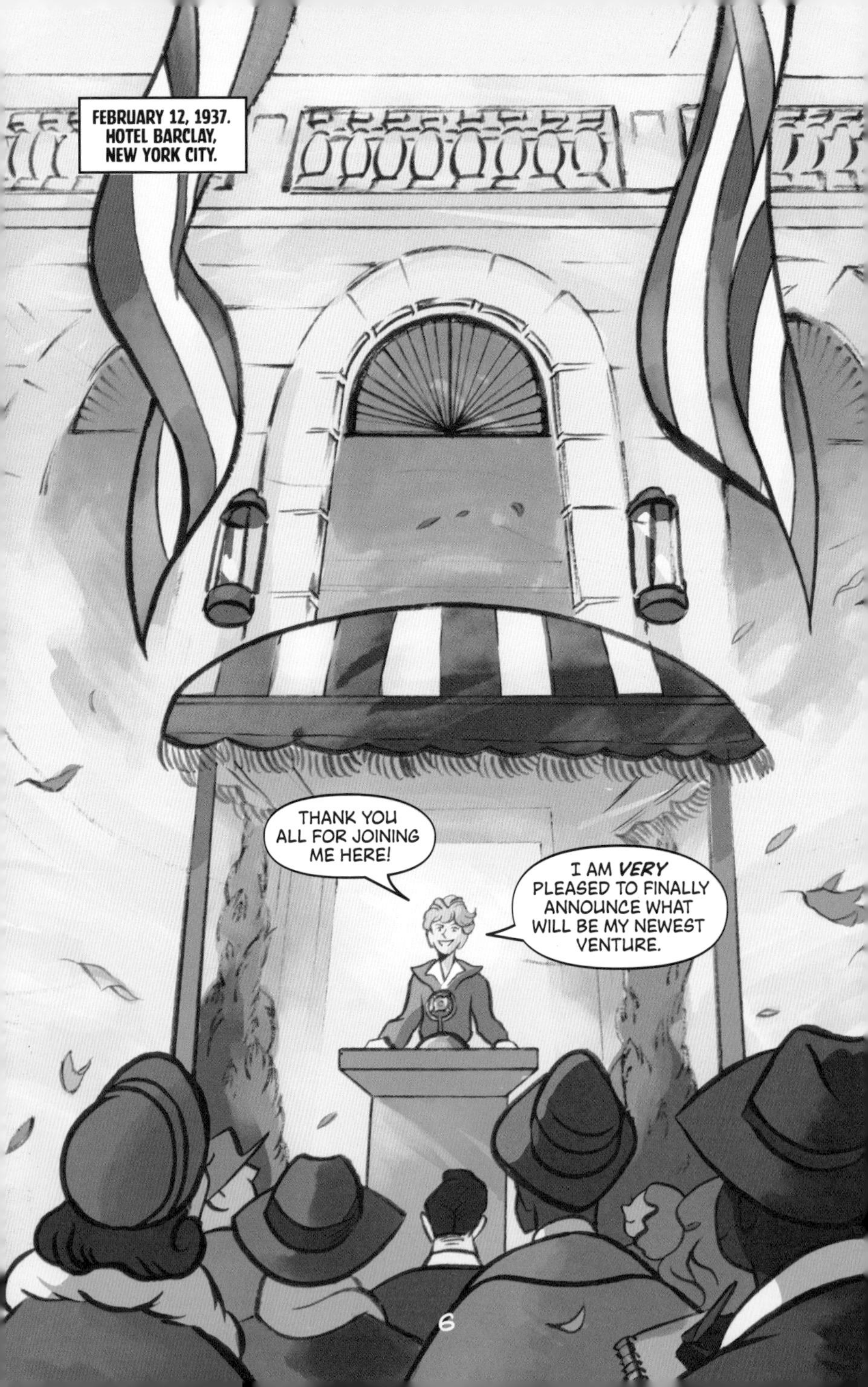
FEBRUARY 12, 1937.
HOTEL BARCLAY,
NEW YORK CITY.
THANK YOU ALL FOR JOINING ME HERE!
I AM VERY PLEASED TO FINALLY ANNOUNCE WHAT WILL BE MY NEWEST VENTURE.

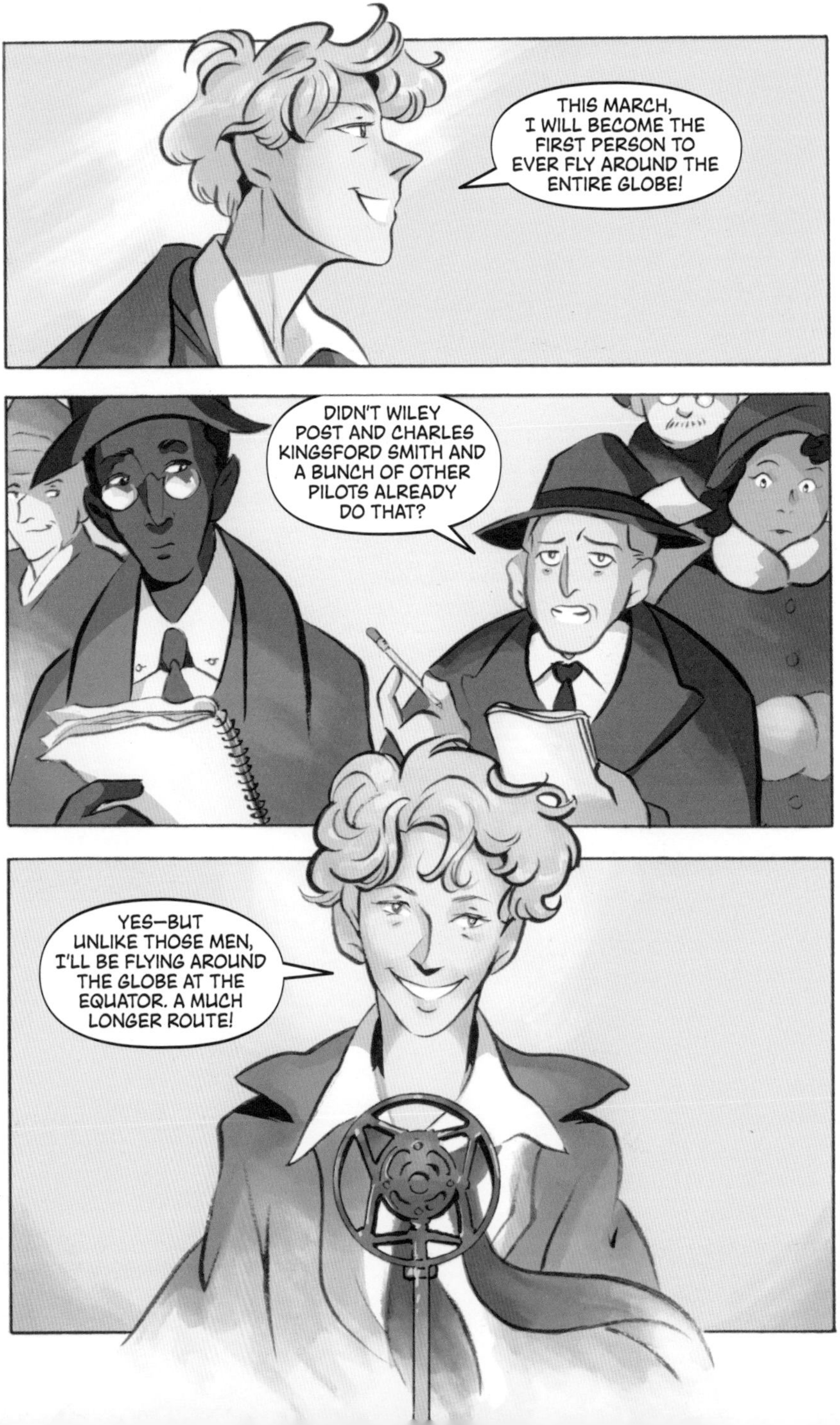
THIS MARCH, I WILL BECOME THE FIRST PERSON TO EVER FLY AROUND THE ENTIRE GLOBE!
DIDN'T WILEY POST AND CHARLES KINGSFORD SMITH AND A BUNCH OF OTHER PILOTS ALREADY DO THAT?
YES—BUT UNLIKE THOSE MEN, I'LL BE FLYING AROUND THE GLOBE AT THE EQUATOR. A MUCH LONGER ROUTE!

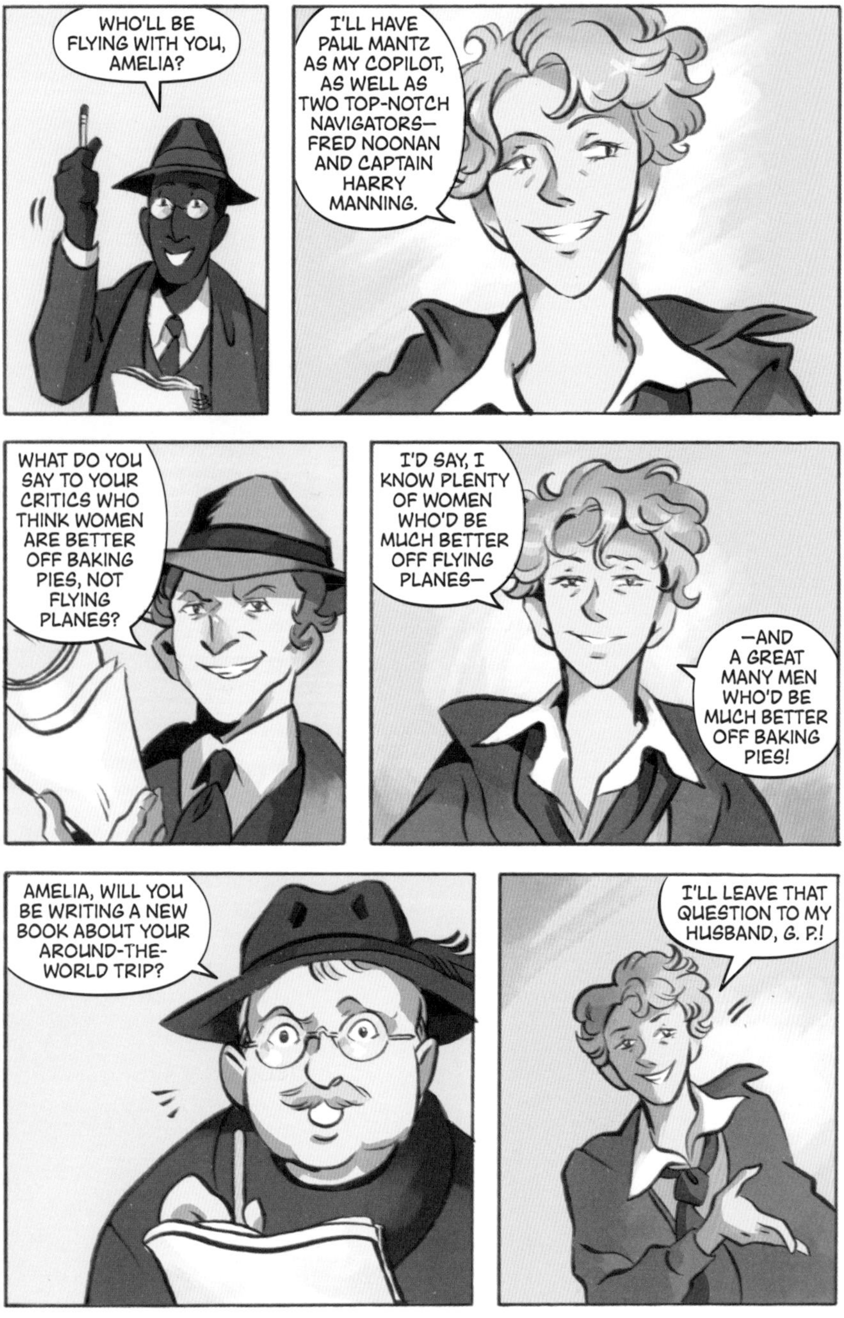
WHO'LL BE FLYING WITH YOU, AMELIA?
I'LL HAVE PAUL MANTZ AS MY COPILOT, AS WELL AS TWO TOP-NOTCH NAVIGATORS—FRED NOONAN AND CAPTAIN HARRY MANNING.
WHAT DO YOU SAY TO YOUR CRITICS WHO THINK WOMEN ARE BETTER OFF BAKING PIES, NOT FLYING PLANES?
I'D SAY, I KNOW PLENTY OF WOMEN WHO'D BE MUCH BETTER OFF FLYING PLANES—
—AND A GREAT MANY MEN WHO'D BE MUCH BETTER OFF BAKING PIES!
AMELIA, WILL YOU BE WRITING A NEW BOOK ABOUT YOUR AROUND-THE-WORLD TRIP?
I'LL LEAVE THAT QUESTION TO MY HUSBAND, G. P.!

Fred Noonan, Captain Harry Manning, and Paul Mantz

Fred Noonan, Captain Harry Manning, and Paul Mantz were three pilots who served as Amelia Earhart's longtime, trusted crew members.

Fred Noonan began his career as a sailor, working first on British merchant ships and then joining the Merchant Marine. In 1930, he earned his pilot's license and began a new career in aviation, working for the airline Pan Am. And in 1937, he agreed to fly with Amelia Earhart on her around-the-world trip, as one of her navigators.

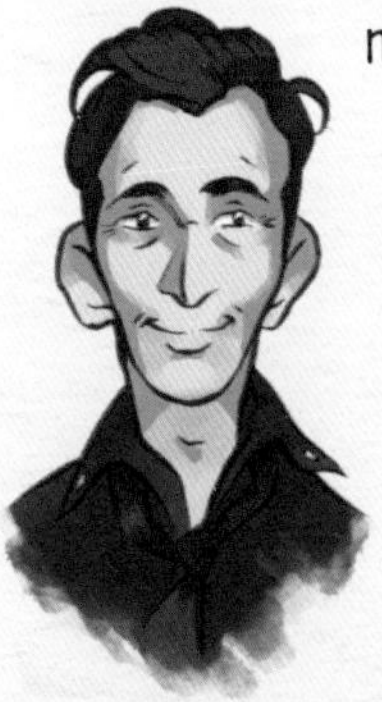

Captain Harry Manning was a highly experienced aviator, mariner, and navigator, and an officer for the US Navy Reserve. Manning was the only member of the four-person flight crew who was skilled as a radio operator—an important navigational tool.

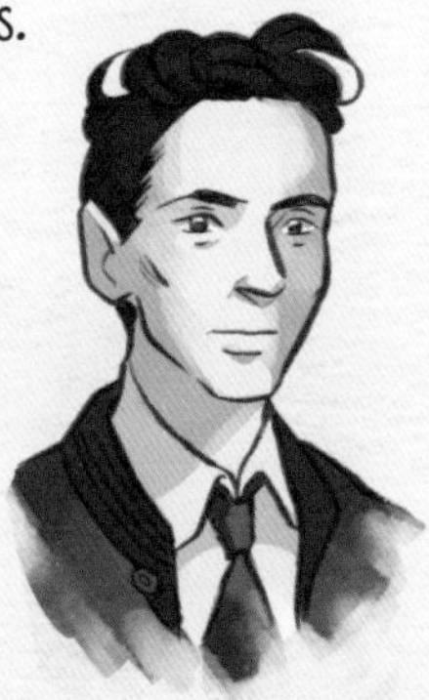

Paul Mantz was a famous air-racing pilot and stunt pilot—and someone who'd tutored Amelia when she was still learning how to fly and navigate long-distance trips. He accompanied Amelia on her first of two attempts to fly around the world.

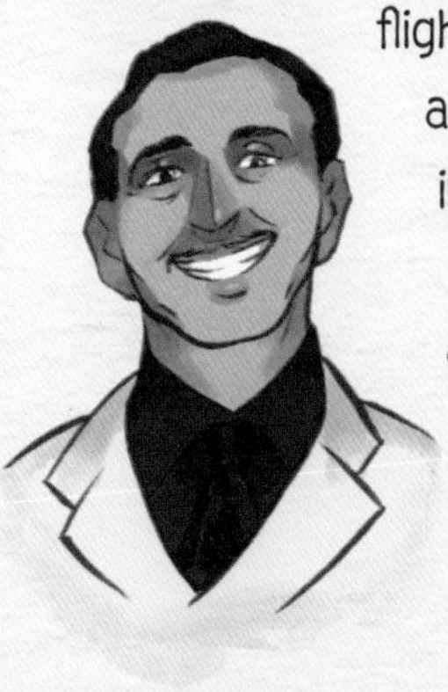

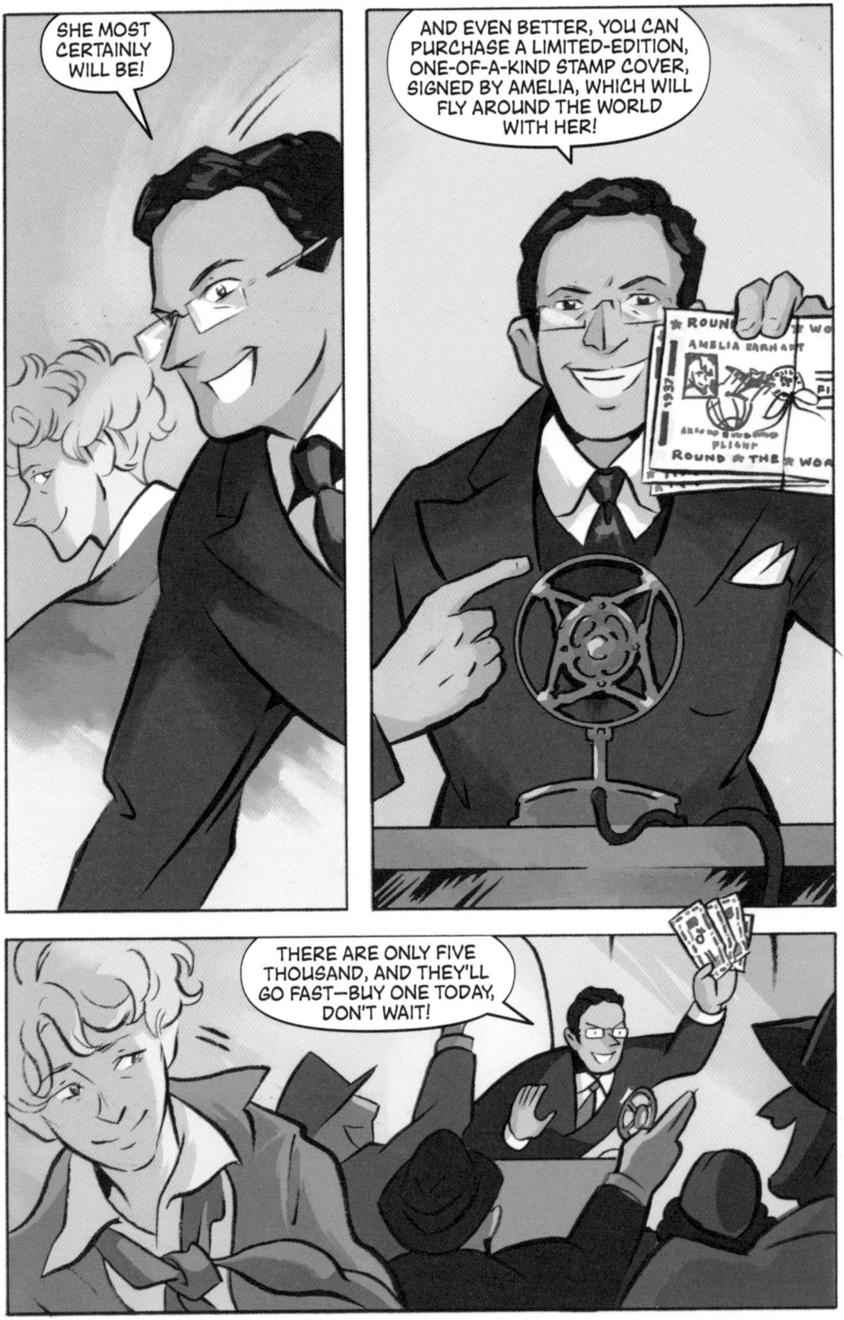
SHE MOST CERTAINLY WILL BE!
AND EVEN BETTER, YOU CAN PURCHASE A LIMITED-EDITION, ONE-OF-A-KIND STAMP COVER, SIGNED BY AMELIA, WHICH WILL FLY AROUND THE WORLD WITH HER!
AMELIA EARHART
FLIGHT
THERE ARE ONLY FIVE THOUSAND, AND THEY'LL GO FAST—BUY ONE TODAY, DON'T WAIT!

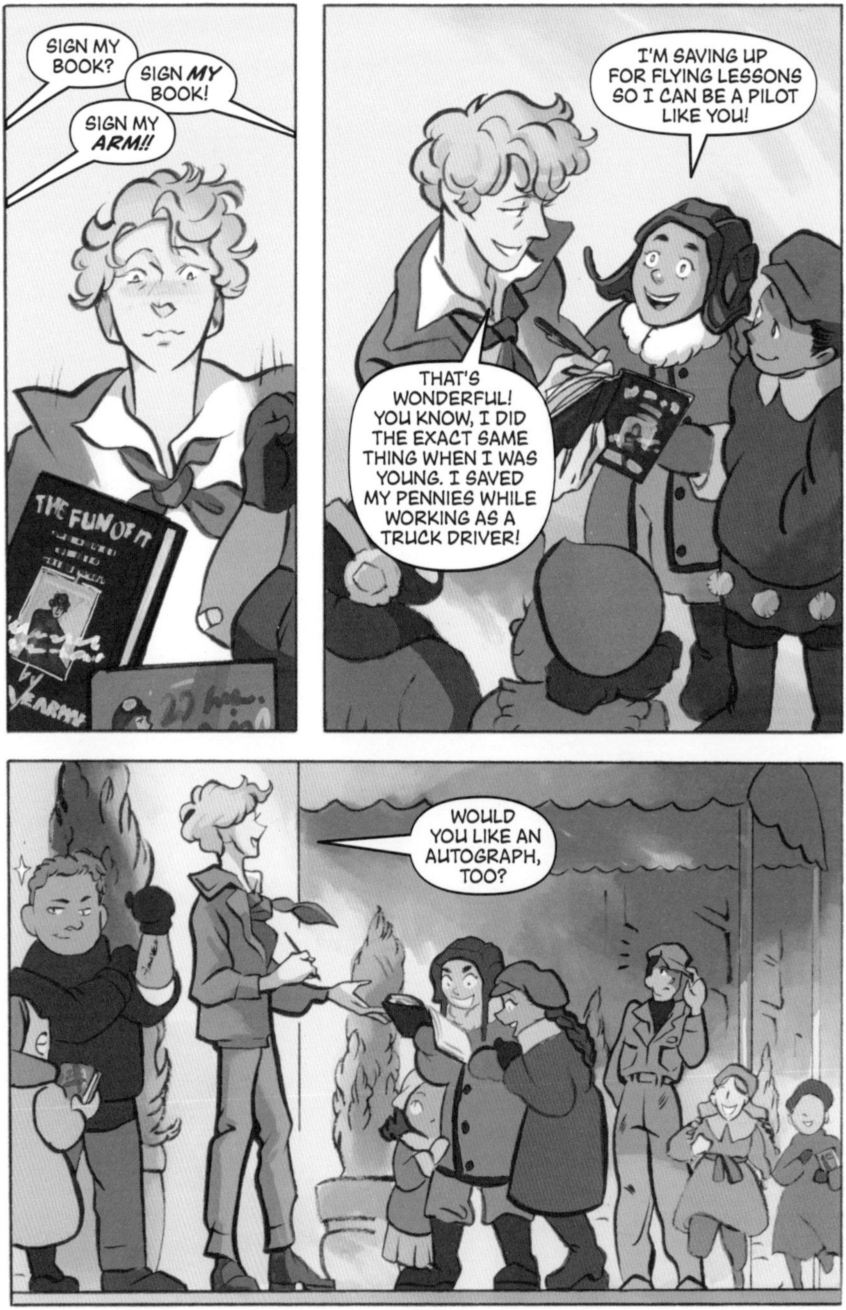
SIGN MY BOOK?
SIGN **MY** BOOK!
SIGN MY **ARM!!**
THE FUN OF IT
I'M SAVING UP FOR FLYING LESSONS SO I CAN BE A PILOT LIKE YOU!
THAT'S WONDERFUL! YOU KNOW, I DID THE EXACT SAME THING WHEN I WAS YOUNG. I SAVED MY PENNIES WHILE WORKING AS A TRUCK DRIVER!
WOULD YOU LIKE AN AUTOGRAPH, TOO?

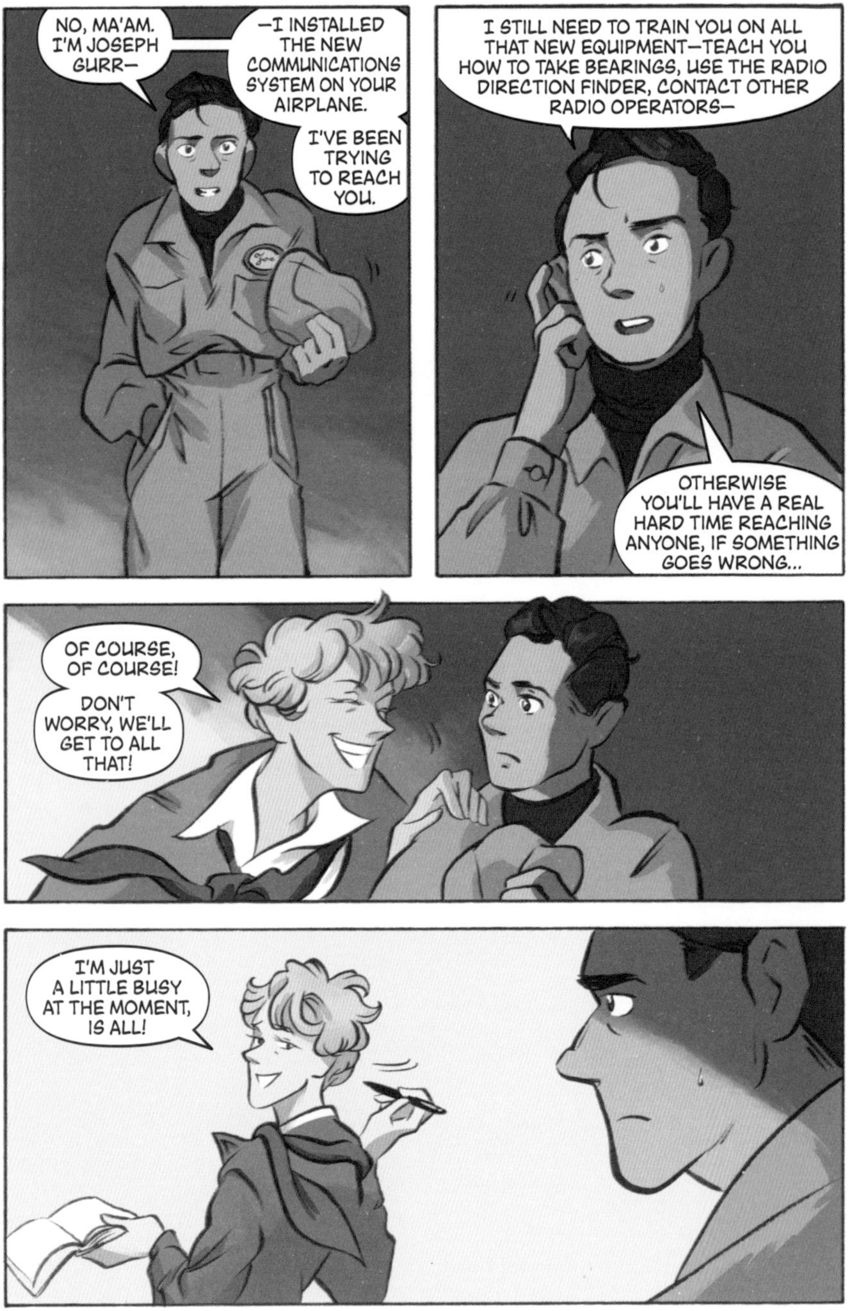
NO, MA'AM. I'M JOSEPH GURR—
—I INSTALLED THE NEW COMMUNICATIONS SYSTEM ON YOUR AIRPLANE.
I'VE BEEN TRYING TO REACH YOU.
I STILL NEED TO TRAIN YOU ON ALL THAT NEW EQUIPMENT—TEACH YOU HOW TO TAKE BEARINGS, USE THE RADIO DIRECTION FINDER, CONTACT OTHER RADIO OPERATORS—
OTHERWISE YOU'LL HAVE A REAL HARD TIME REACHING ANYONE, IF SOMETHING GOES WRONG...
OF COURSE, OF COURSE!
DON'T WORRY, WE'LL GET TO ALL THAT!
I'M JUST A LITTLE BUSY AT THE MOMENT, IS ALL!

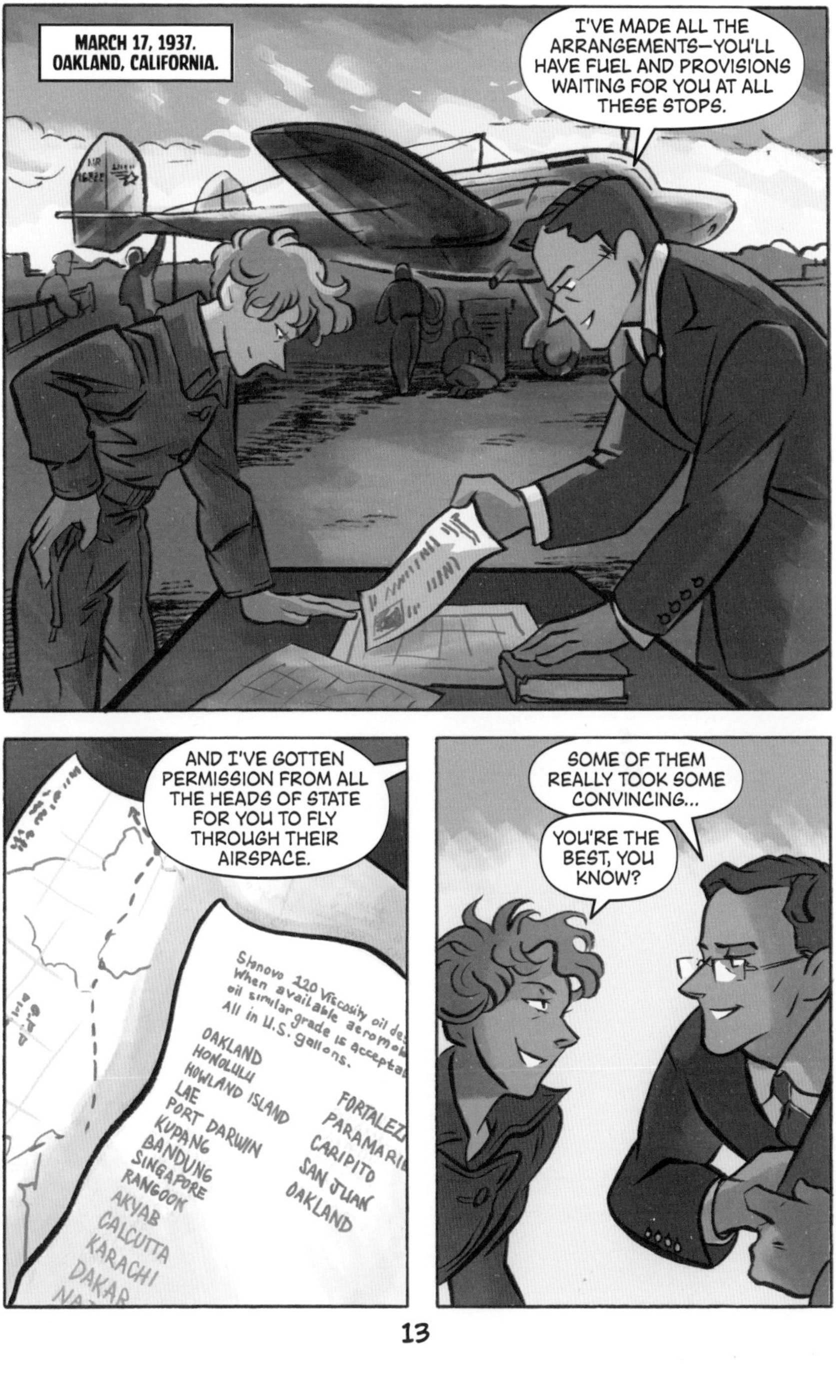
MARCH 17, 1937.
OAKLAND, CALIFORNIA.
I'VE MADE ALL THE ARRANGEMENTS—YOU'LL HAVE FUEL AND PROVISIONS WAITING FOR YOU AT ALL THESE STOPS.
AND I'VE GOTTEN PERMISSION FROM ALL THE HEADS OF STATE FOR YOU TO FLY THROUGH THEIR AIRSPACE.
All in U.S. gallons.
OAKLAND
HONOLULU
HOWLAND ISLAND
LAE
PORT DARWIN
KUPANG
BANDUNG
SINGAPORE
RANGOON
AKYAB
CALCUTTA
KARACHI
DAKAR
CARIPITO
SAN JUAN
OAKLAND
SOME OF THEM REALLY TOOK SOME CONVINCING...
YOU'RE THE BEST, YOU KNOW?

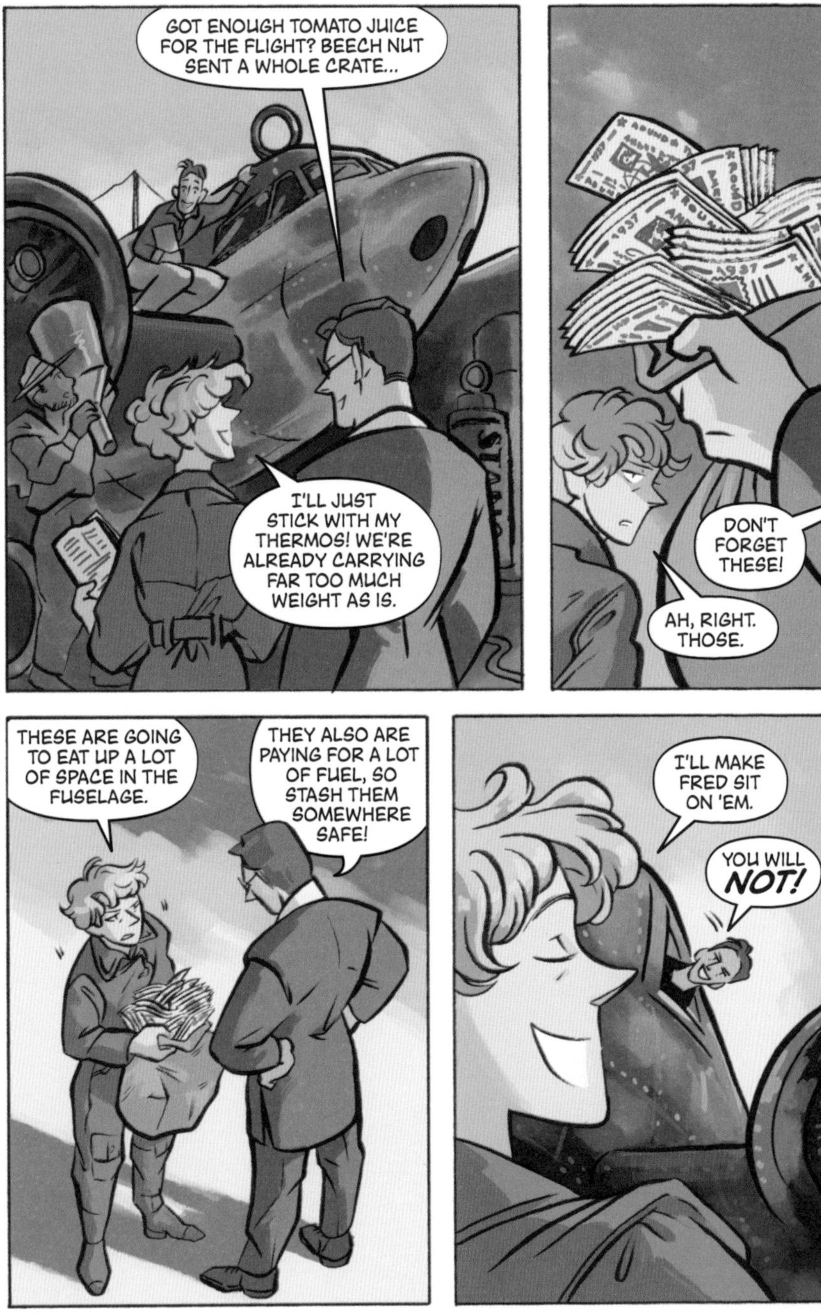
GOT ENOUGH TOMATO JUICE FOR THE FLIGHT? BEECH NUT SENT A WHOLE CRATE...
I'LL JUST STICK WITH MY THERMOS! WE'RE ALREADY CARRYING FAR TOO MUCH WEIGHT AS IS.
DON'T FORGET THESE!
AH, RIGHT. THOSE.
THESE ARE GOING TO EAT UP A LOT OF SPACE IN THE FUSELAGE.
THEY ALSO ARE PAYING FOR A LOT OF FUEL, SO STASH THEM SOMEWHERE SAFE!
I'LL MAKE FRED SIT ON 'EM.
YOU WILL ***NOT!***

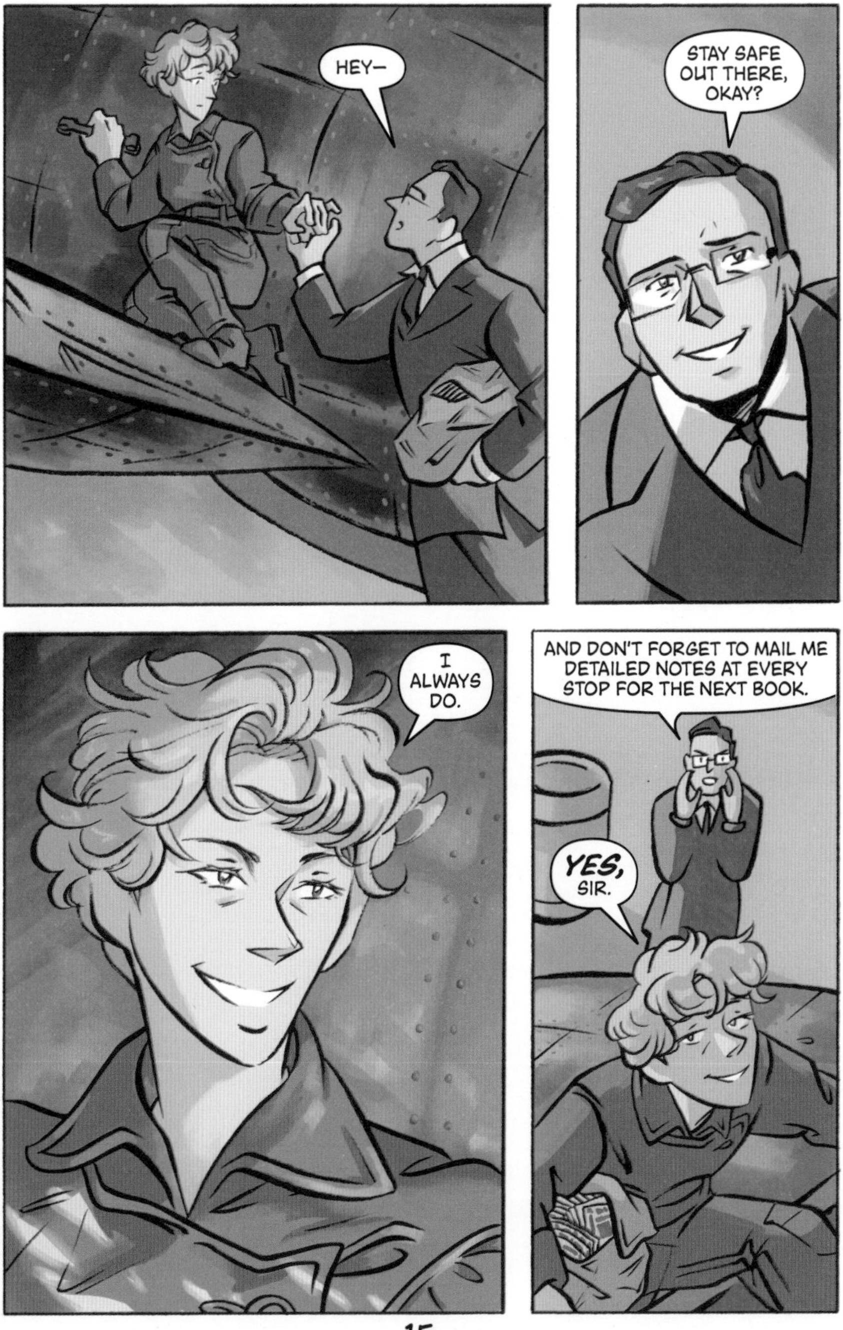
HEY—
STAY SAFE OUT THERE, OKAY?
I ALWAYS DO.
AND DON'T FORGET TO MAIL ME DETAILED NOTES AT EVERY STOP FOR THE NEXT BOOK.
YES, SIR.

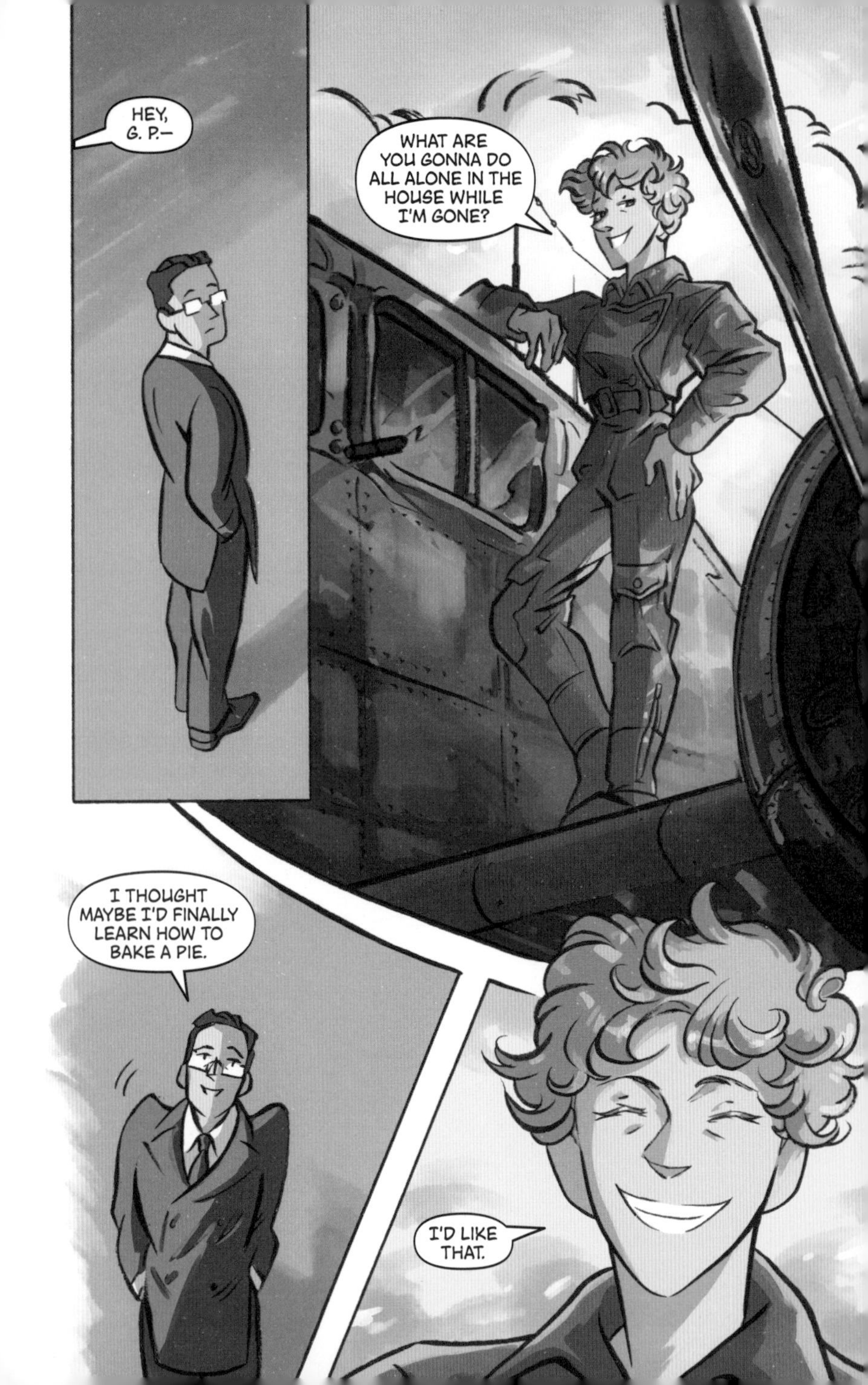
HEY, G. P.—
WHAT ARE YOU GONNA DO ALL ALONE IN THE HOUSE WHILE I'M GONE?
I THOUGHT MAYBE I'D FINALLY LEARN HOW TO BAKE A PIE.
I'D LIKE THAT.

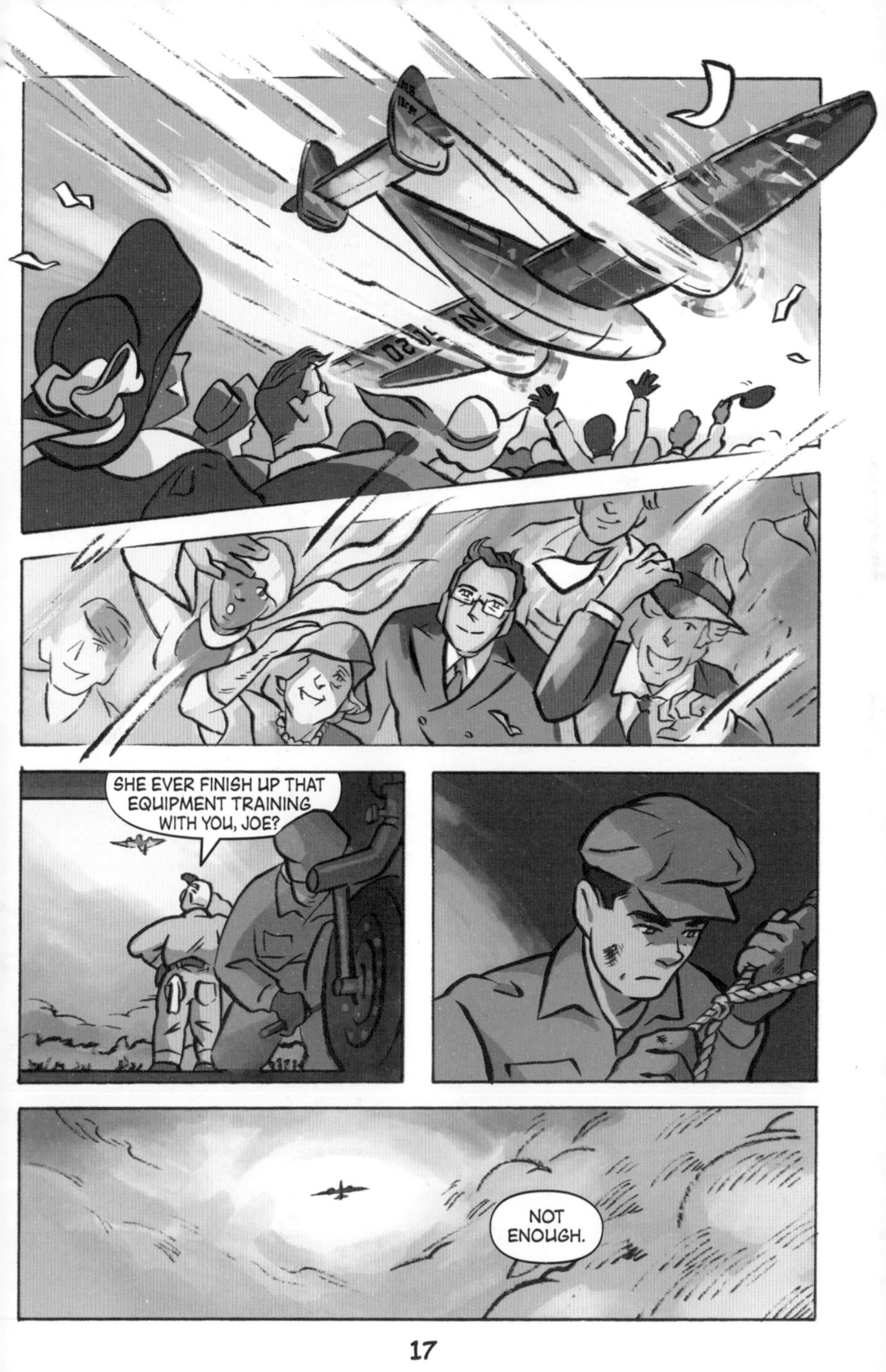
SHE EVER FINISH UP THAT EQUIPMENT TRAINING WITH YOU, JOE?
NOT ENOUGH.

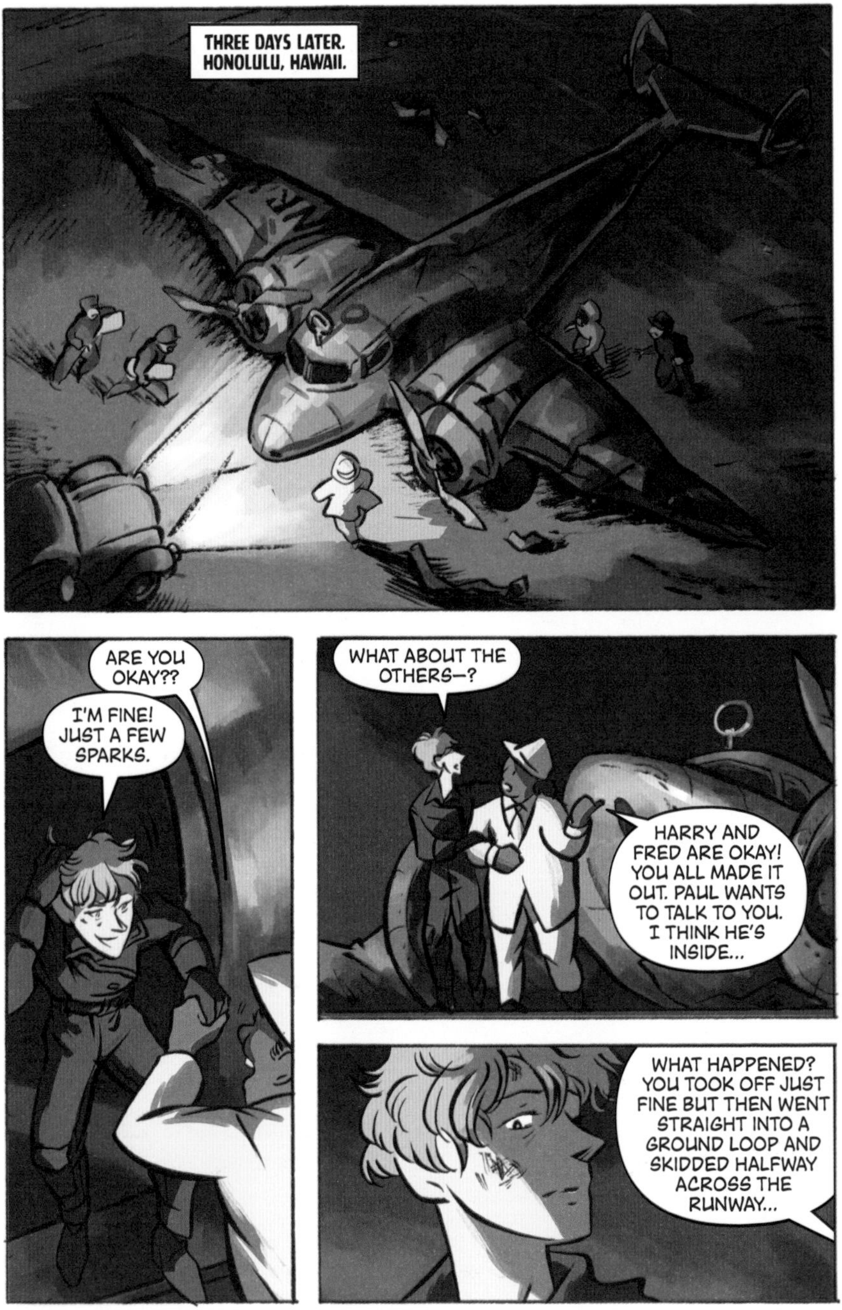
THREE DAYS LATER. HONOLULU, HAWAII.
ARE YOU OKAY??
I'M FINE! JUST A FEW SPARKS.
WHAT ABOUT THE OTHERS—?
HARRY AND FRED ARE OKAY! YOU ALL MADE IT OUT. PAUL WANTS TO TALK TO YOU. I THINK HE'S INSIDE...
WHAT HAPPENED? YOU TOOK OFF JUST FINE BUT THEN WENT STRAIGHT INTO A GROUND LOOP AND SKIDDED HALFWAY ACROSS THE RUNWAY...

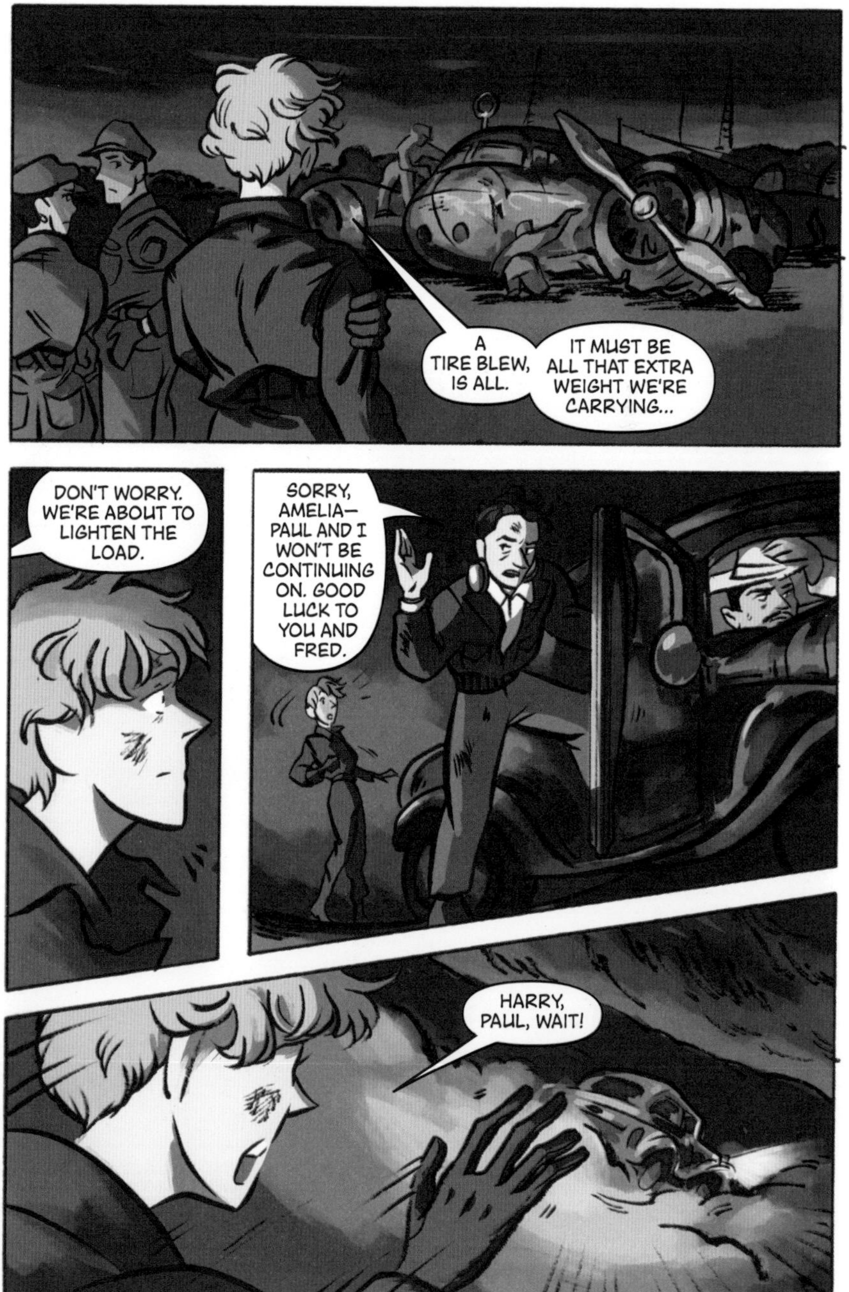
A TIRE BLEW, IS ALL.
IT MUST BE ALL THAT EXTRA WEIGHT WE'RE CARRYING...
DON'T WORRY. WE'RE ABOUT TO LIGHTEN THE LOAD.
SORRY, AMELIA— PAUL AND I WON'T BE CONTINUING ON. GOOD LUCK TO YOU AND FRED.
HARRY, PAUL, WAIT!

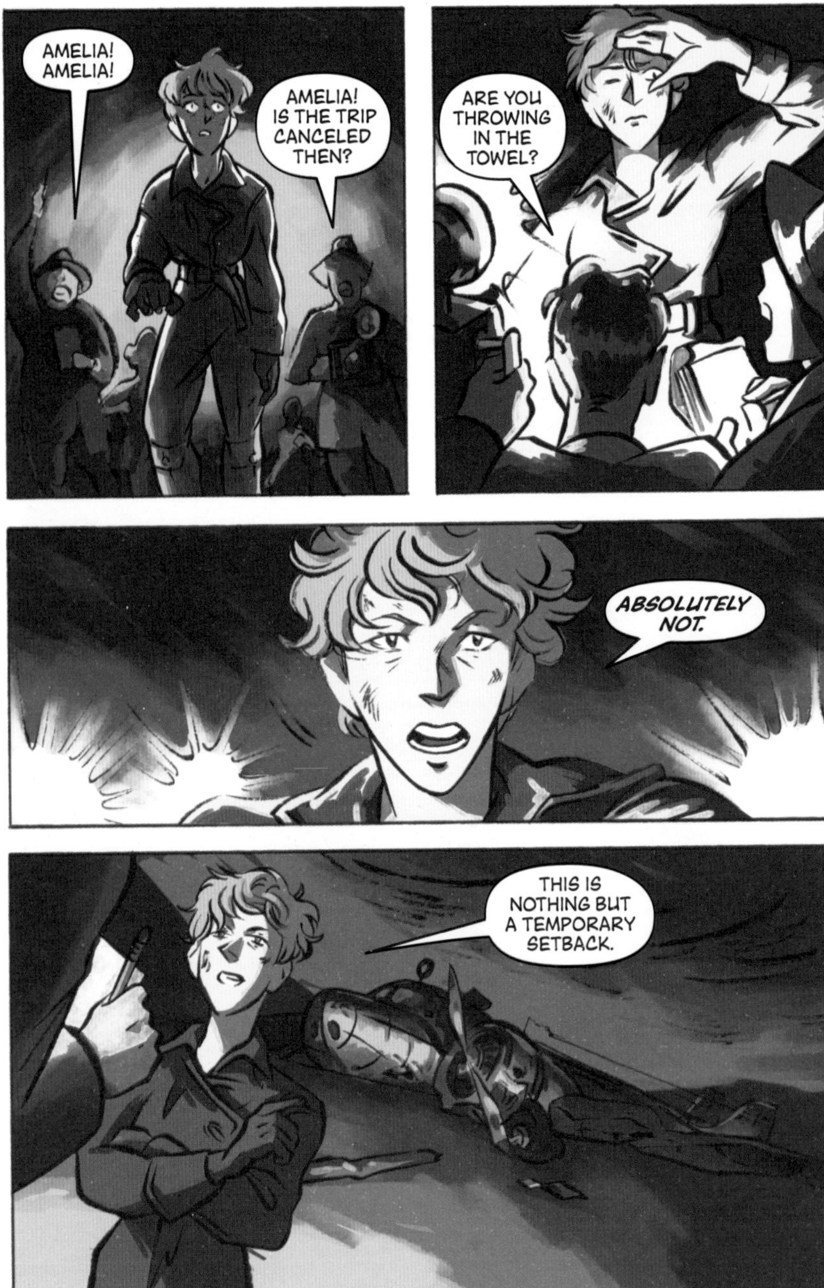
AMELIA! AMELIA!
AMELIA! IS THE TRIP CANCELED THEN?
ARE YOU THROWING IN THE TOWEL?
ABSOLUTELY NOT.
THIS IS NOTHING BUT A TEMPORARY SETBACK.

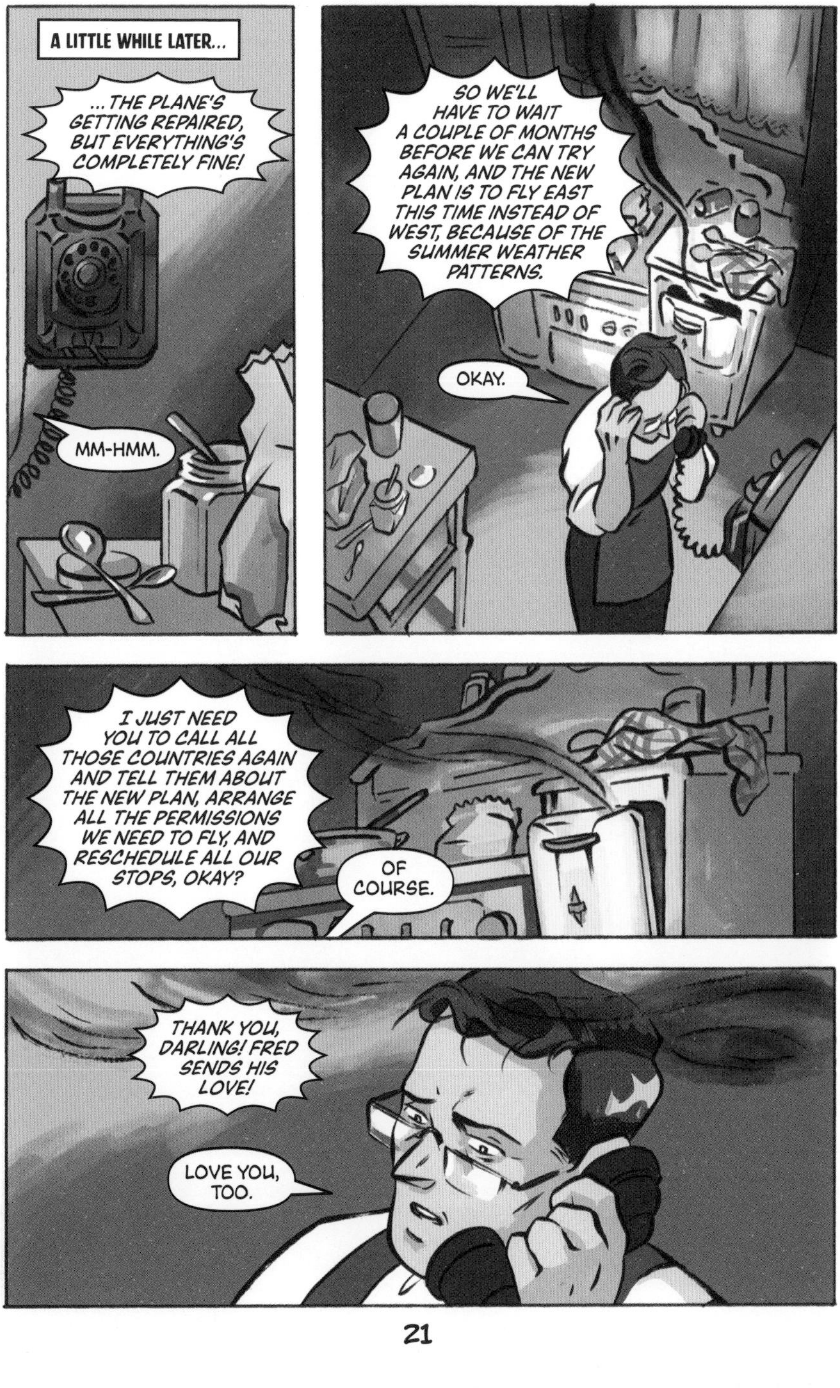
A LITTLE WHILE LATER...
...THE PLANE'S GETTING REPAIRED, BUT EVERYTHING'S COMPLETELY FINE!
MM-HMM.
SO WE'LL HAVE TO WAIT A COUPLE OF MONTHS BEFORE WE CAN TRY AGAIN, AND THE NEW PLAN IS TO FLY EAST THIS TIME INSTEAD OF WEST, BECAUSE OF THE SUMMER WEATHER PATTERNS.
OKAY.
I JUST NEED YOU TO CALL ALL THOSE COUNTRIES AGAIN AND TELL THEM ABOUT THE NEW PLAN, ARRANGE ALL THE PERMISSIONS WE NEED TO FLY, AND RESCHEDULE ALL OUR STOPS, OKAY?
OF COURSE.
THANK YOU, DARLING! FRED SENDS HIS LOVE!
LOVE YOU, TOO.

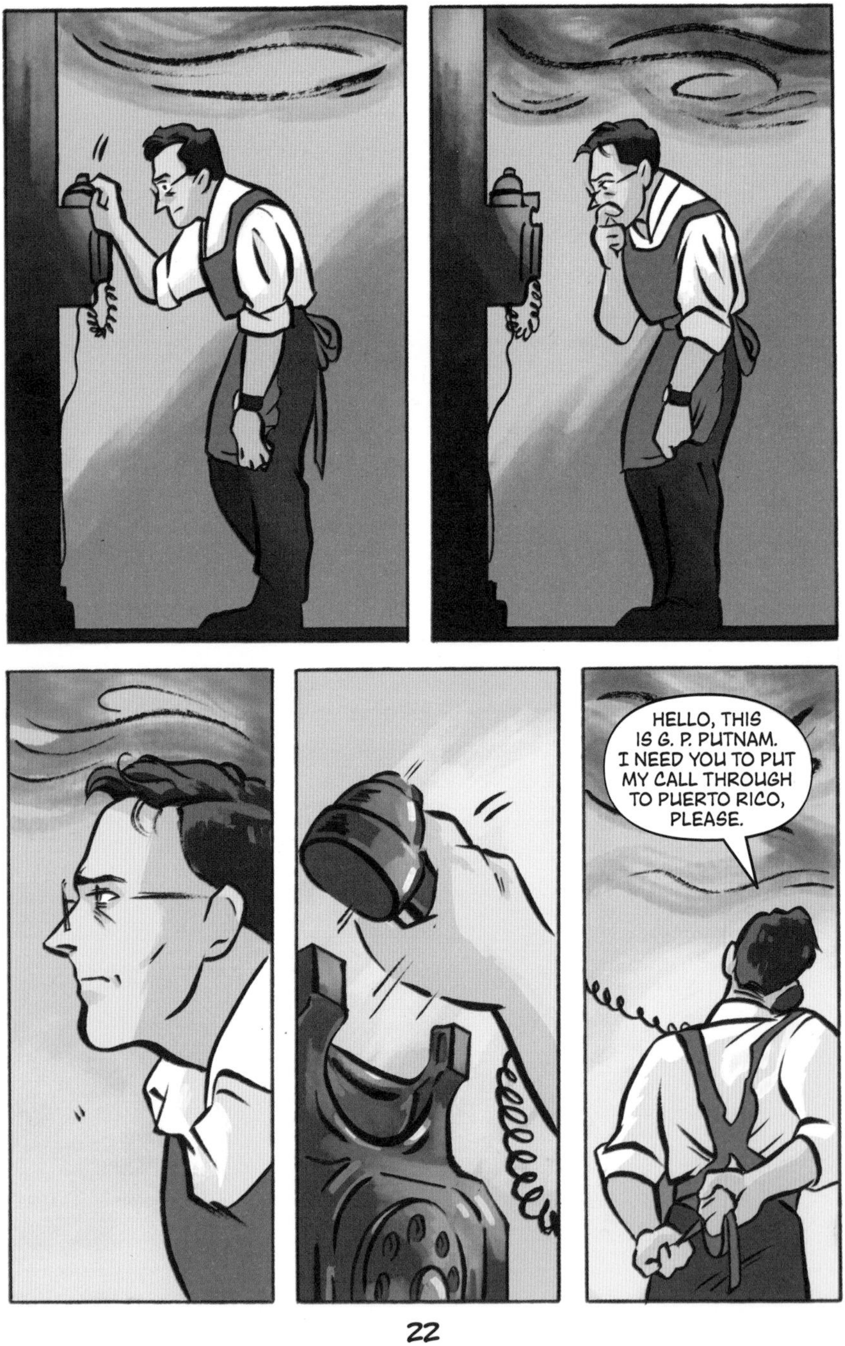
HELLO, THIS IS G. P. PUTNAM. I NEED YOU TO PUT MY CALL THROUGH TO PUERTO RICO, PLEASE.

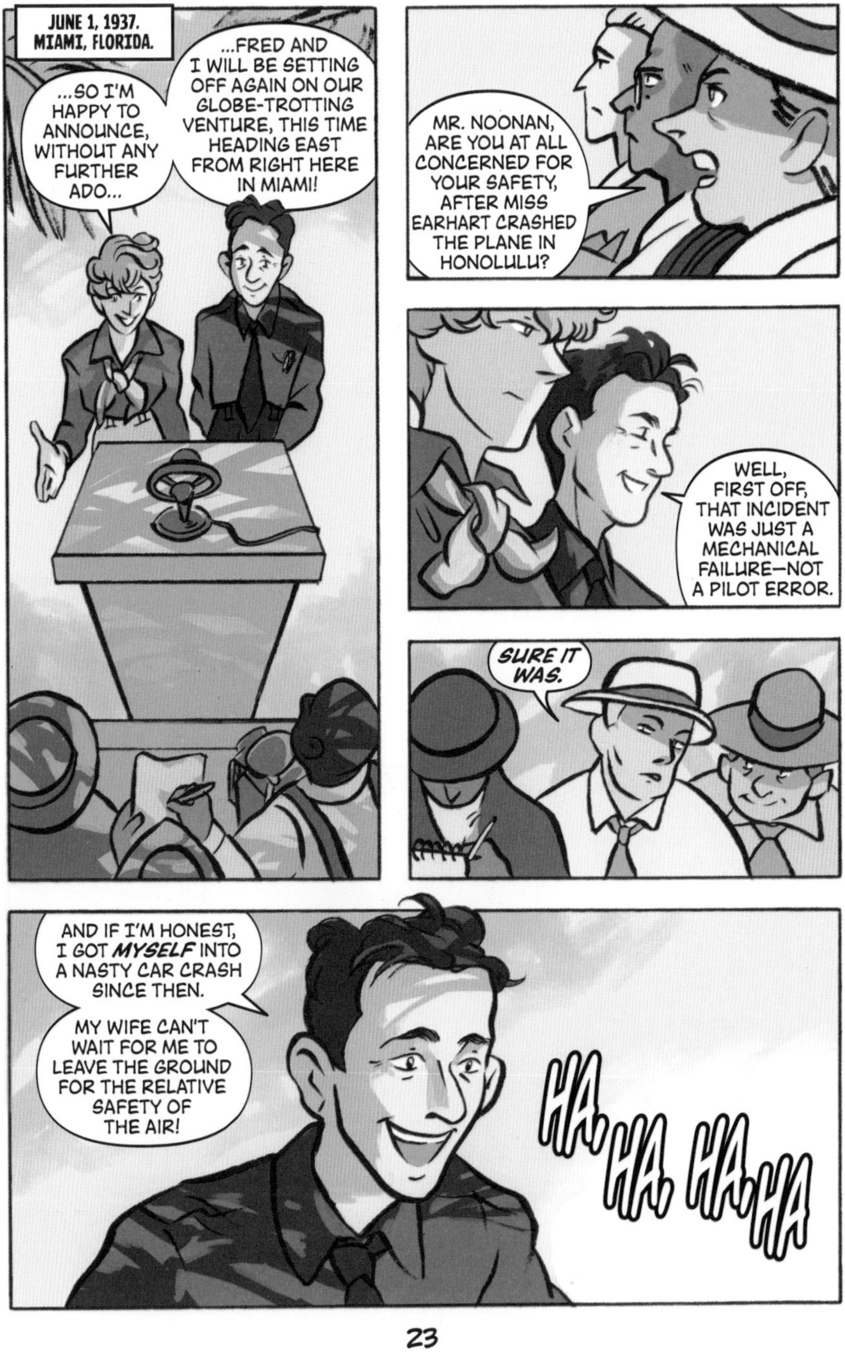
JUNE 1, 1937. MIAMI, FLORIDA.
...SO I'M HAPPY TO ANNOUNCE, WITHOUT ANY FURTHER ADO...
...FRED AND I WILL BE SETTING OFF AGAIN ON OUR GLOBE-TROTTING VENTURE, THIS TIME HEADING EAST FROM RIGHT HERE IN MIAMI!
MR. NOONAN, ARE YOU AT ALL CONCERNED FOR YOUR SAFETY, AFTER MISS EARHART CRASHED THE PLANE IN HONOLULU?
WELL, FIRST OFF, THAT INCIDENT WAS JUST A MECHANICAL FAILURE—NOT A PILOT ERROR.
SURE IT WAS.
AND IF I'M HONEST, I GOT MYSELF INTO A NASTY CAR CRASH SINCE THEN.
MY WIFE CAN'T WAIT FOR ME TO LEAVE THE GROUND FOR THE RELATIVE SAFETY OF THE AIR!
HA, HA, HA, HA

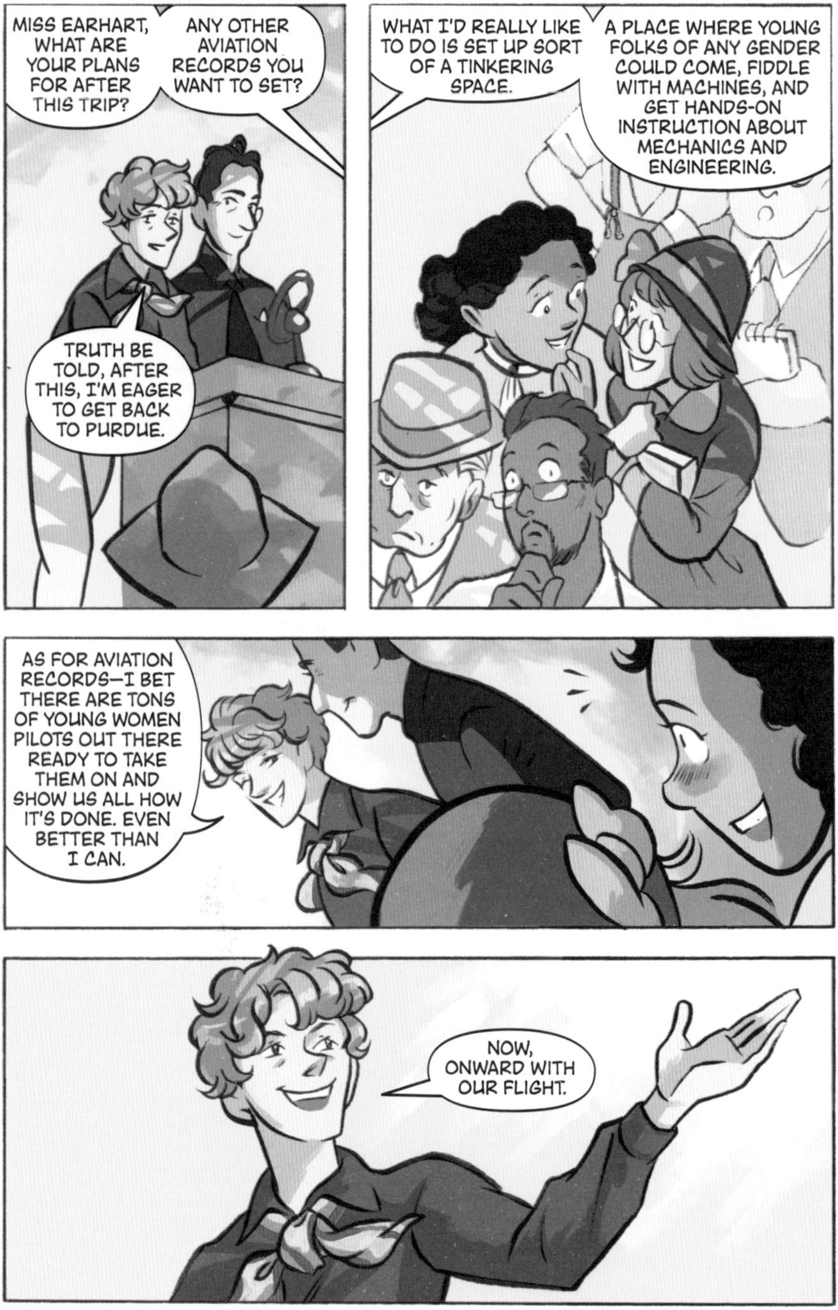
MISS EARHART, WHAT ARE YOUR PLANS FOR AFTER THIS TRIP?
ANY OTHER AVIATION RECORDS YOU WANT TO SET?
TRUTH BE TOLD, AFTER THIS, I'M EAGER TO GET BACK TO PURDUE.
WHAT I'D REALLY LIKE TO DO IS SET UP SORT OF A TINKERING SPACE.
A PLACE WHERE YOUNG FOLKS OF ANY GENDER COULD COME, FIDDLE WITH MACHINES, AND GET HANDS-ON INSTRUCTION ABOUT MECHANICS AND ENGINEERING.
AS FOR AVIATION RECORDS—I BET THERE ARE TONS OF YOUNG WOMEN PILOTS OUT THERE READY TO TAKE THEM ON AND SHOW US ALL HOW IT'S DONE. EVEN BETTER THAN I CAN.
NOW, ONWARD WITH OUR FLIGHT.

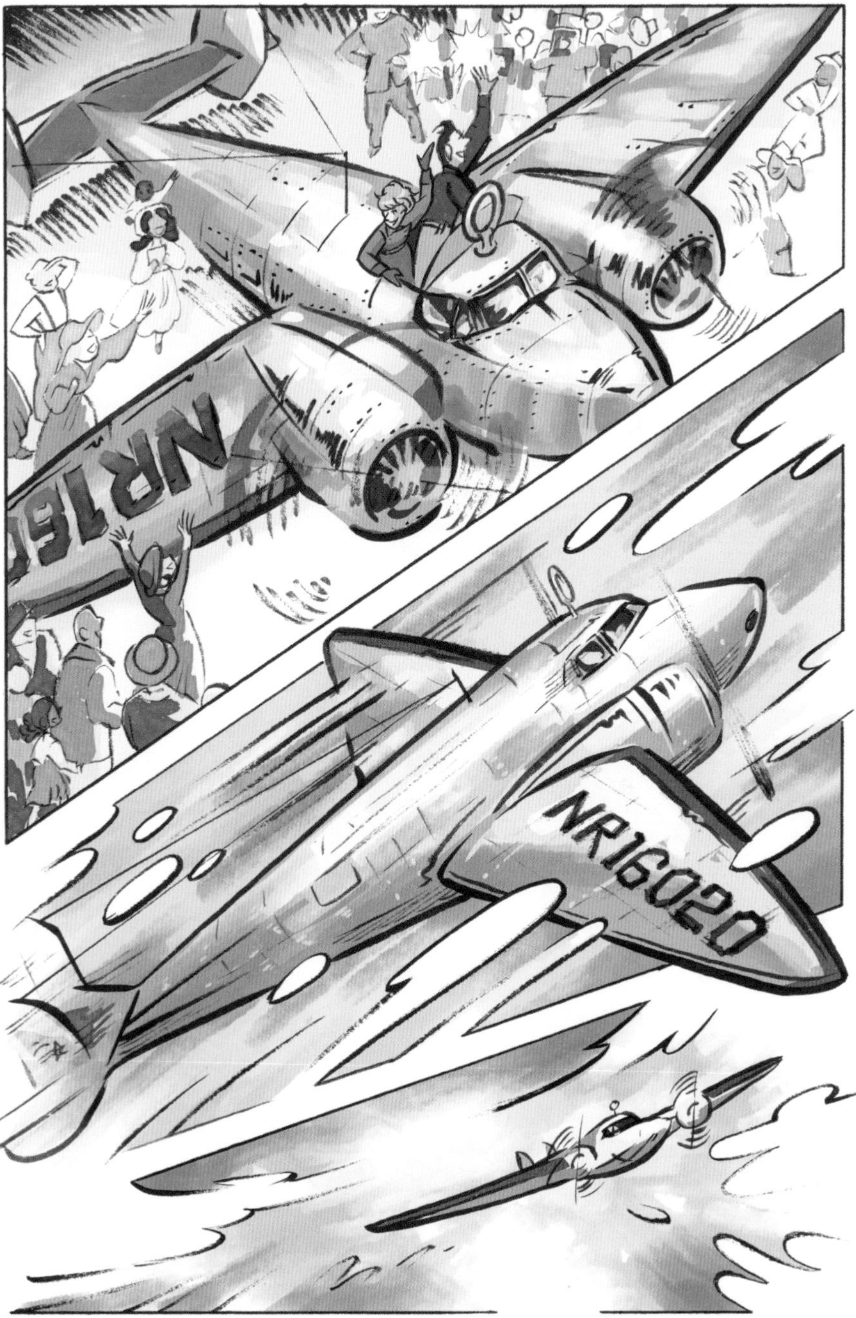
NR16020

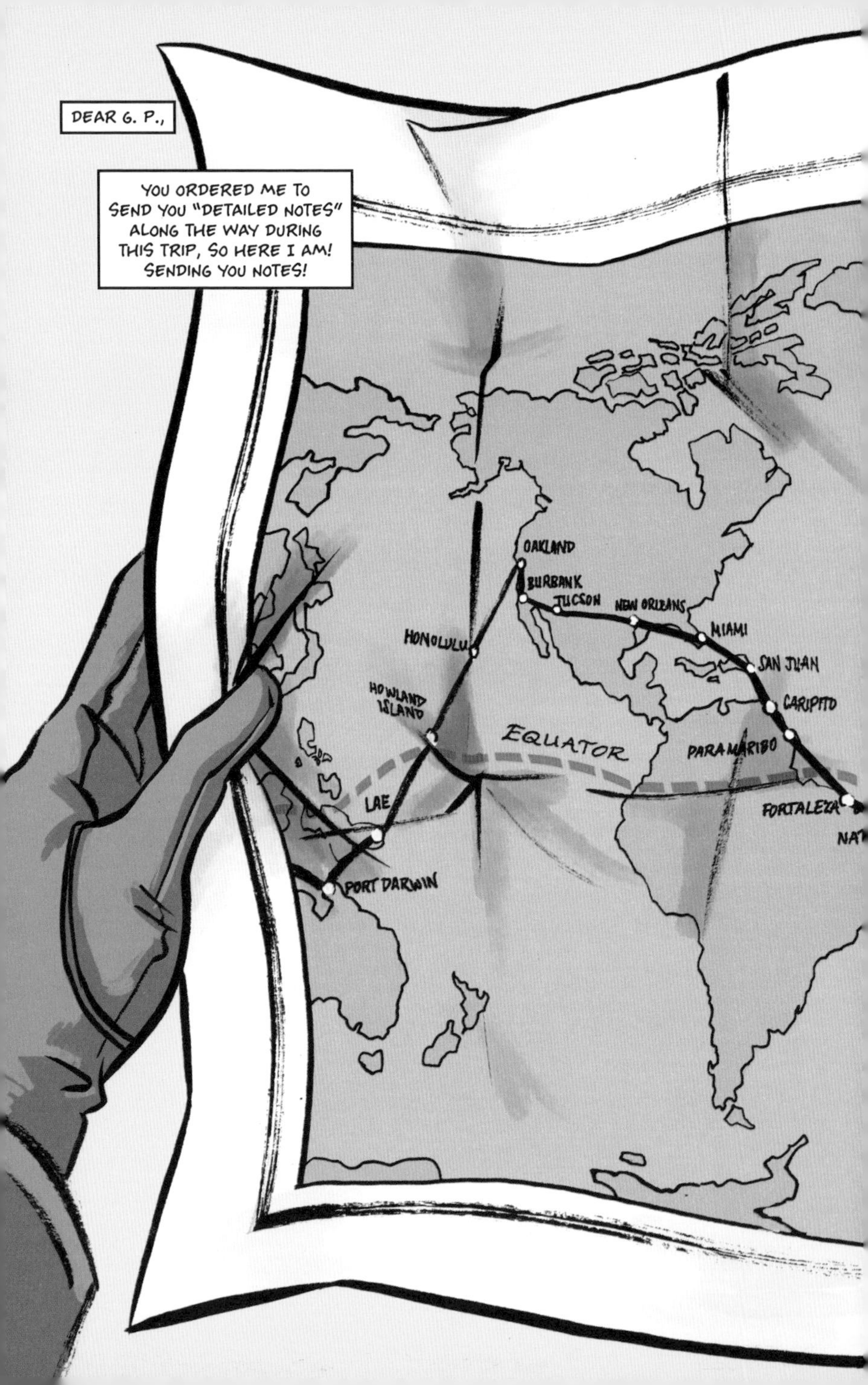
DEAR G. P.,
YOU ORDERED ME TO SEND YOU "DETAILED NOTES" ALONG THE WAY DURING THIS TRIP, SO HERE I AM! SENDING YOU NOTES!
OAKLAND
BURBANK
TUCSON
NEW ORLEANS
MIAMI
SAN JUAN
CARIPITO
PARAMARIBO
FORTALEZA
HONOLULU
HOWLAND ISLAND
EQUATOR
LAE
PORT DARWIN

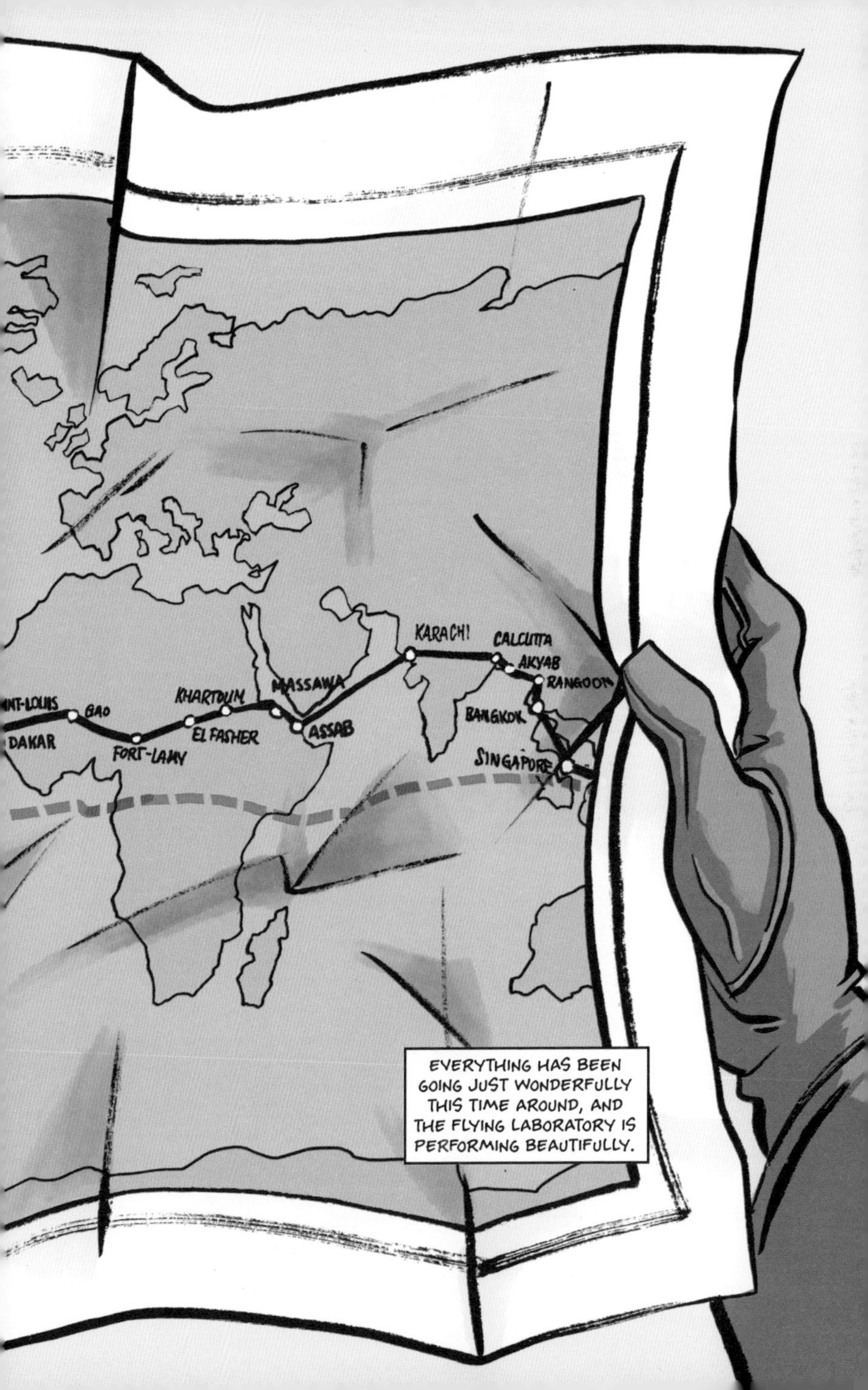
NT-LOUIS
DAKAR
GAO
FORT-LAMY
EL FASHER
KHARTOUM
MASSAWA
ASSAB
KARACHI
CALCUTTA
AKYAB
RANGOON
BANGKOK
SINGAPORE
EVERYTHING HAS BEEN GOING JUST WONDERFULLY THIS TIME AROUND, AND THE FLYING LABORATORY IS PERFORMING BEAUTIFULLY.

Amelia's Flying Laboratory

In order to make it all the way around the world, Amelia would need a top-notch airplane! But a plane that good would be expensive. Amelia managed to convince Purdue University to donate $50,000 and give her a shiny new silver-and-red Lockheed 10-E Electra. Purdue thought Amelia's flight around the world would, in fact, be important aeronautical research—a field of study the school was interested in. To assist in her research, Purdue outfitted the Electra with a lot of extra scientific equipment—like empty canisters so Amelia could take samples of air during her flight and bring them back for analysis in Purdue's labs. Amelia also had her plane outfitted with a few other modifications—such as room for extra fuel tanks so the plane could travel longer distances without stopping. Because of all the research equipment aboard, Amelia nicknamed her airplane a "flying laboratory."

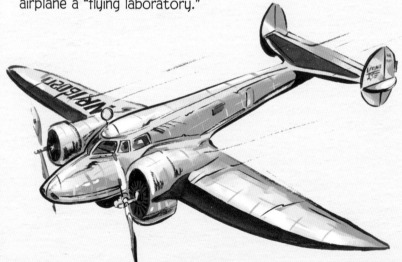

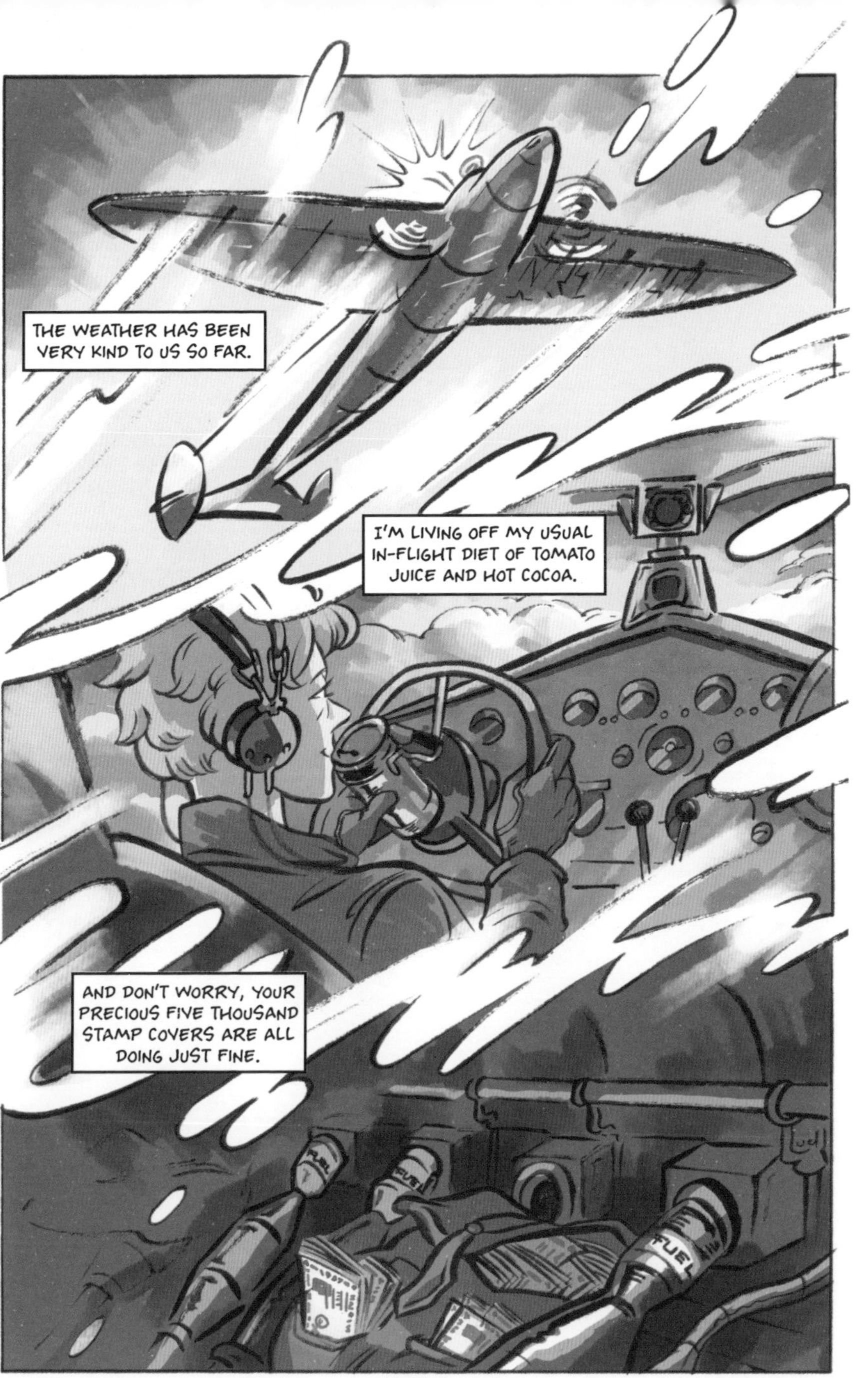
THE WEATHER HAS BEEN VERY KIND TO US SO FAR.
I'M LIVING OFF MY USUAL IN-FLIGHT DIET OF TOMATO JUICE AND HOT COCOA.
AND DON'T WORRY, YOUR PRECIOUS FIVE THOUSAND STAMP COVERS ARE ALL DOING JUST FINE.
FUEL
FUEL
FUEL

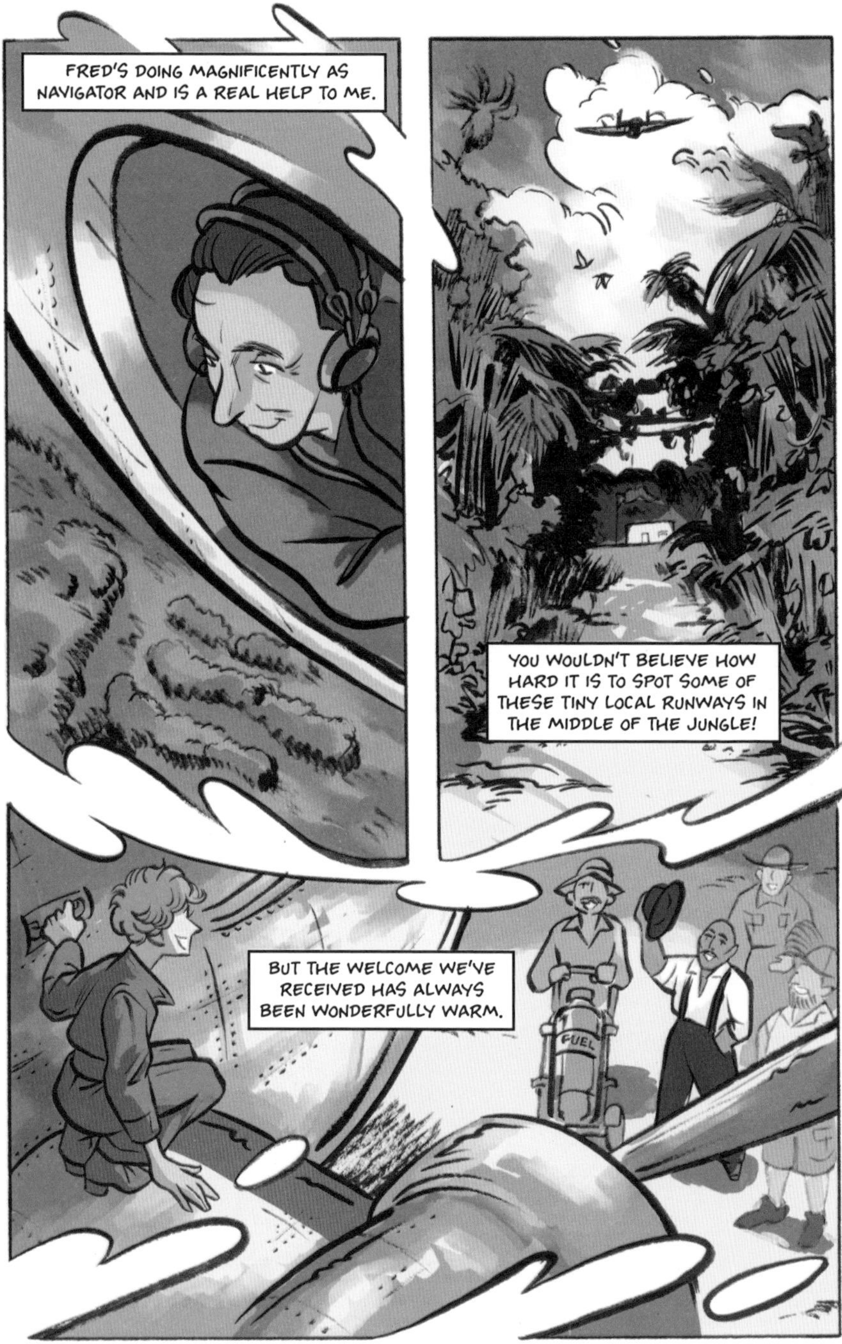
FRED'S DOING MAGNIFICENTLY AS NAVIGATOR AND IS A REAL HELP TO ME.
YOU WOULDN'T BELIEVE HOW HARD IT IS TO SPOT SOME OF THESE TINY LOCAL RUNWAYS IN THE MIDDLE OF THE JUNGLE!
BUT THE WELCOME WE'VE RECEIVED HAS ALWAYS BEEN WONDERFULLY WARM.
FUEL

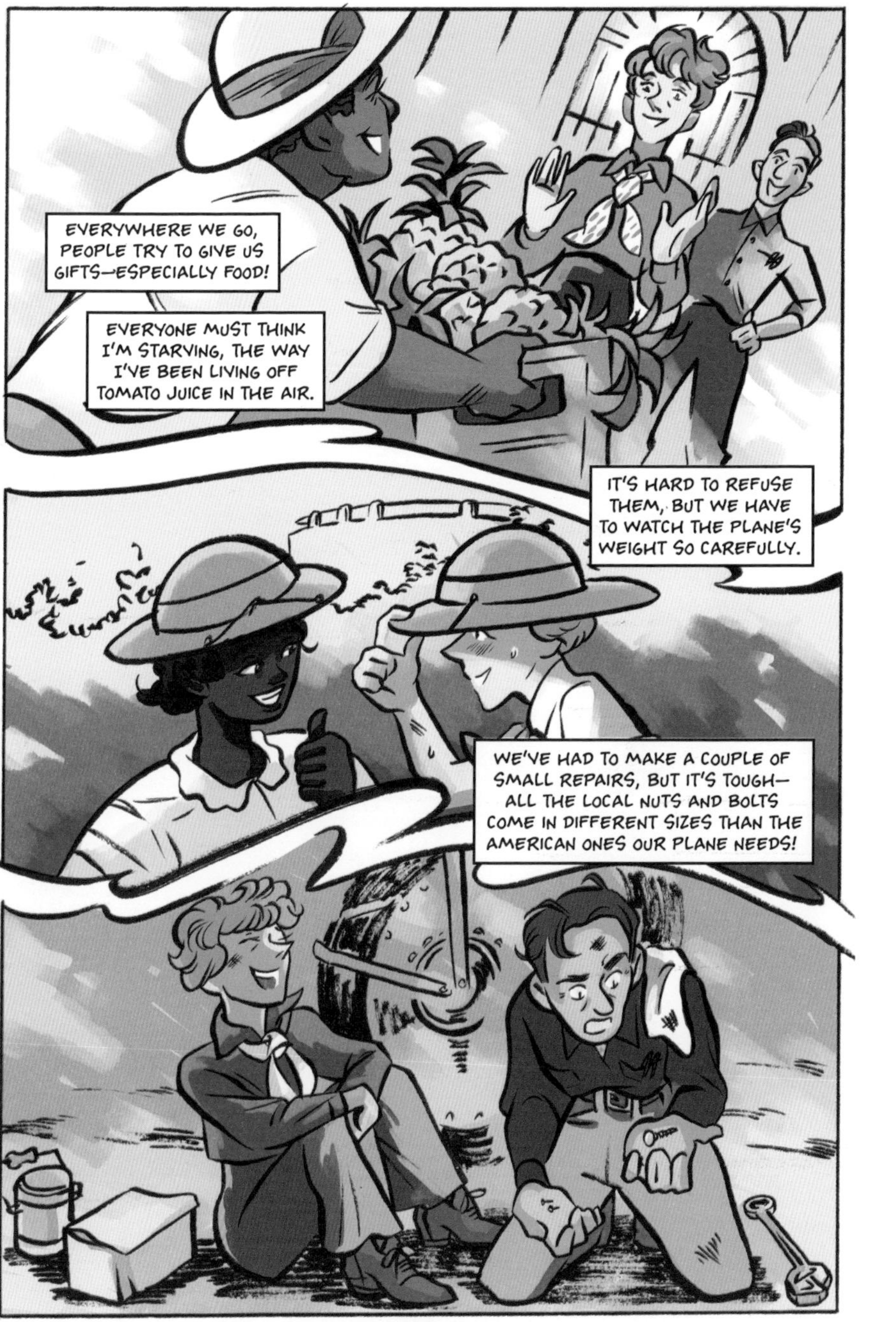
EVERYWHERE WE GO, PEOPLE TRY TO GIVE US GIFTS—ESPECIALLY FOOD!
EVERYONE MUST THINK I'M STARVING, THE WAY I'VE BEEN LIVING OFF TOMATO JUICE IN THE AIR.
IT'S HARD TO REFUSE THEM, BUT WE HAVE TO WATCH THE PLANE'S WEIGHT SO CAREFULLY.
WE'VE HAD TO MAKE A COUPLE OF SMALL REPAIRS, BUT IT'S TOUGH—ALL THE LOCAL NUTS AND BOLTS COME IN DIFFERENT SIZES THAN THE AMERICAN ONES OUR PLANE NEEDS!

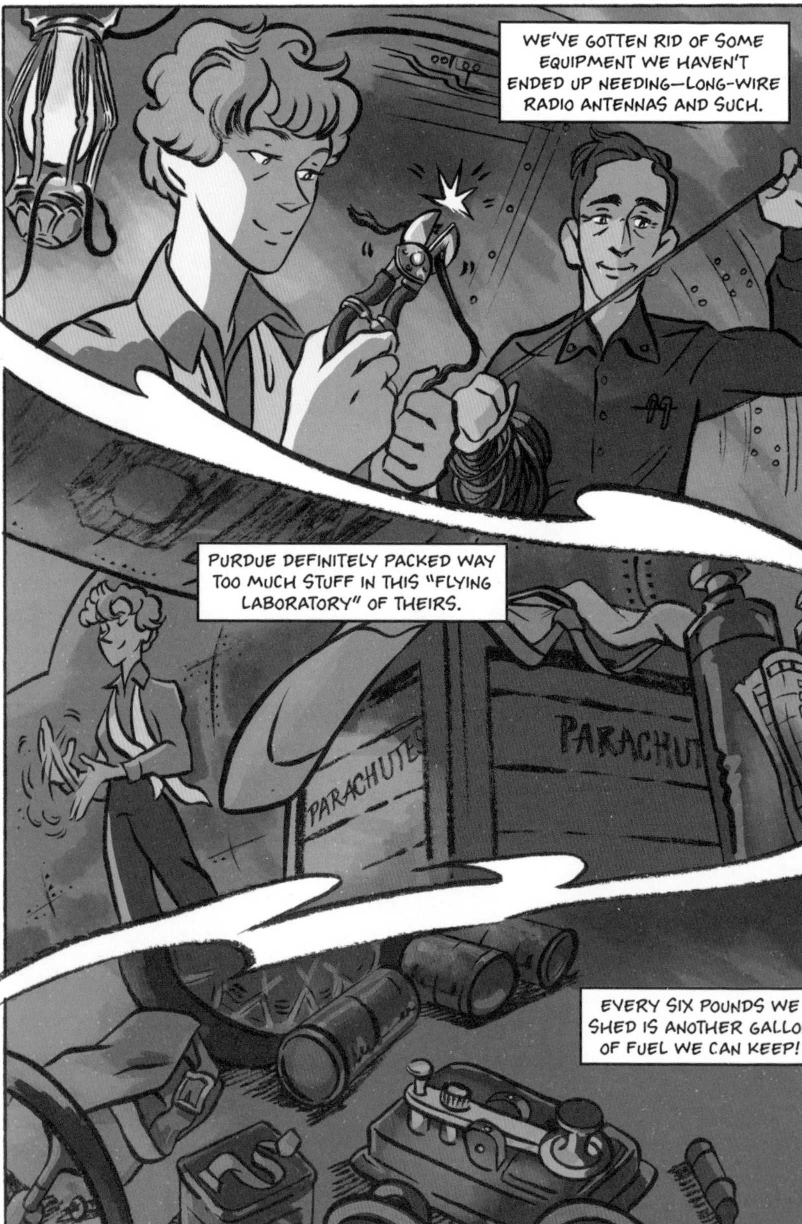
WE'VE GOTTEN RID OF SOME EQUIPMENT WE HAVEN'T ENDED UP NEEDING—LONG-WIRE RADIO ANTENNAS AND SUCH.
PURDUE DEFINITELY PACKED WAY TOO MUCH STUFF IN THIS "FLYING LABORATORY" OF THEIRS.
PARACHUTES
PARACHUT
EVERY SIX POUNDS WE SHED IS ANOTHER GALLON OF FUEL WE CAN KEEP!

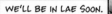

WE'LL BE IN LAE SOON.

THEN IT'S TIME FOR THE HARDEST LEG OF THE JOURNEY, THE TRIP TO HOWLAND—A TINY SPECK OF AN ISLAND IN THE MIDDLE OF THE PACIFIC.

TRY NOT TO WORRY TOO MUCH ABOUT US, THOUGH, DEAR. WE'VE MADE IT THROUGH WORSE!

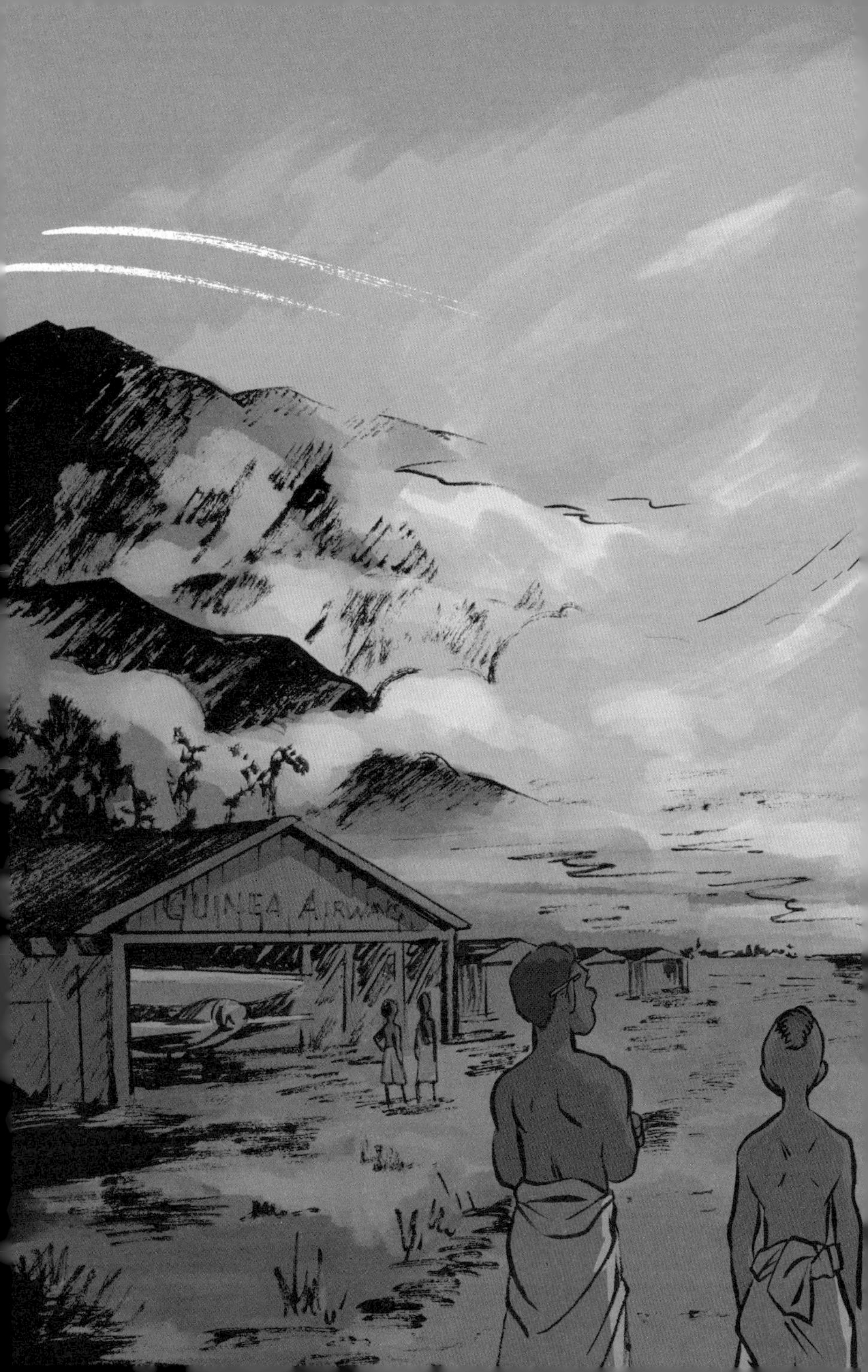
GUINEA AIRWAYS

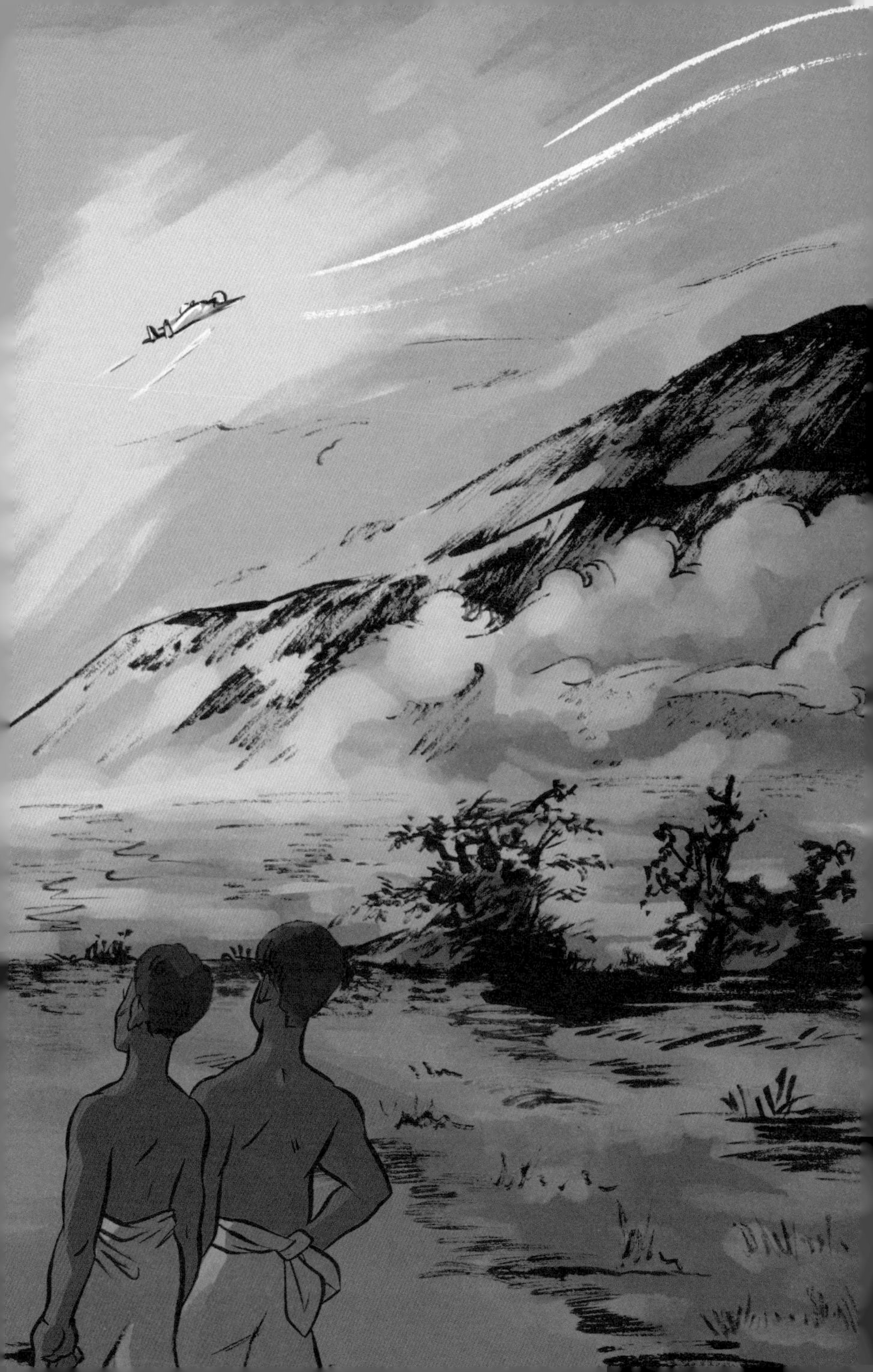

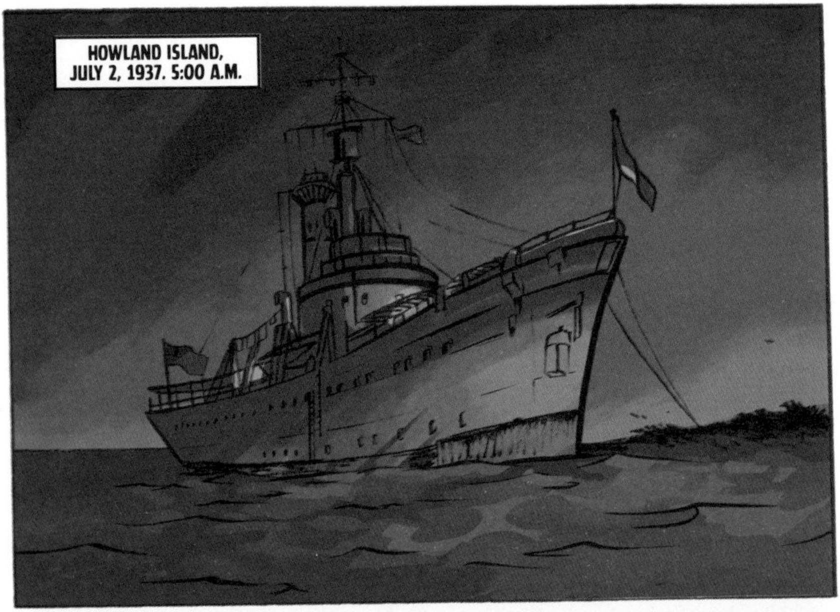
HOWLAND ISLAND,
JULY 2, 1937. 5:00 A.M.

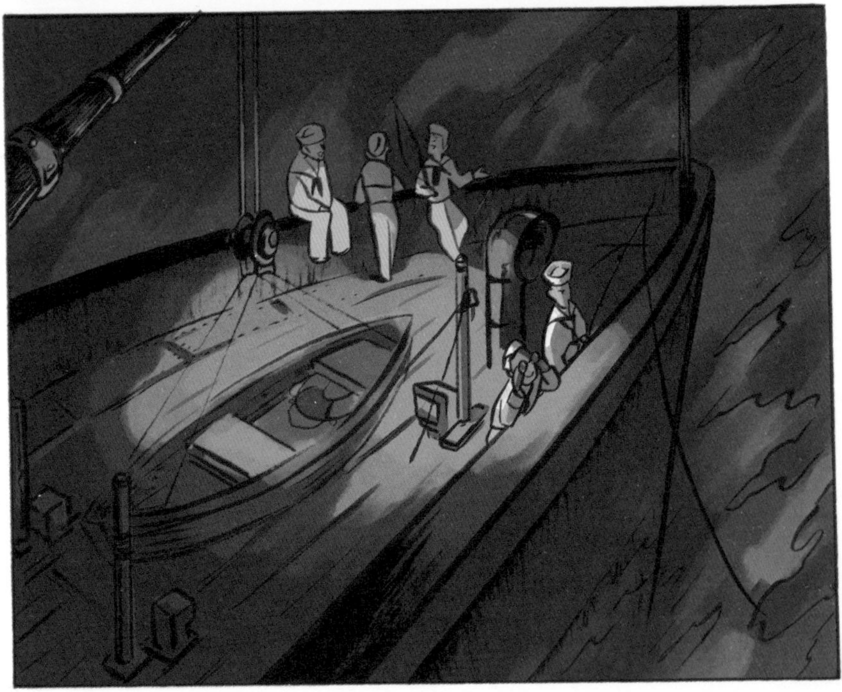

Howland Island

Howland Island is a tiny, uninhabited coral island in the Pacific Ocean, nearly halfway between Australia and Hawaii. The island is about two miles long and half a mile wide—with just barely enough room to build a runway! Because such a tiny island would be incredibly difficult to spot from the air, a ship called the USCGC *Itasca* was waiting for Amelia near the island, ready to help her navigate her way across the ocean.

PACIFIC
OCEAN
OAKLAND
HONOLULU
HOWLAND
LAE

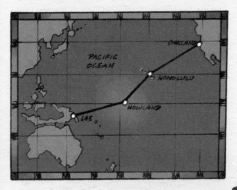

Amelia's planned route

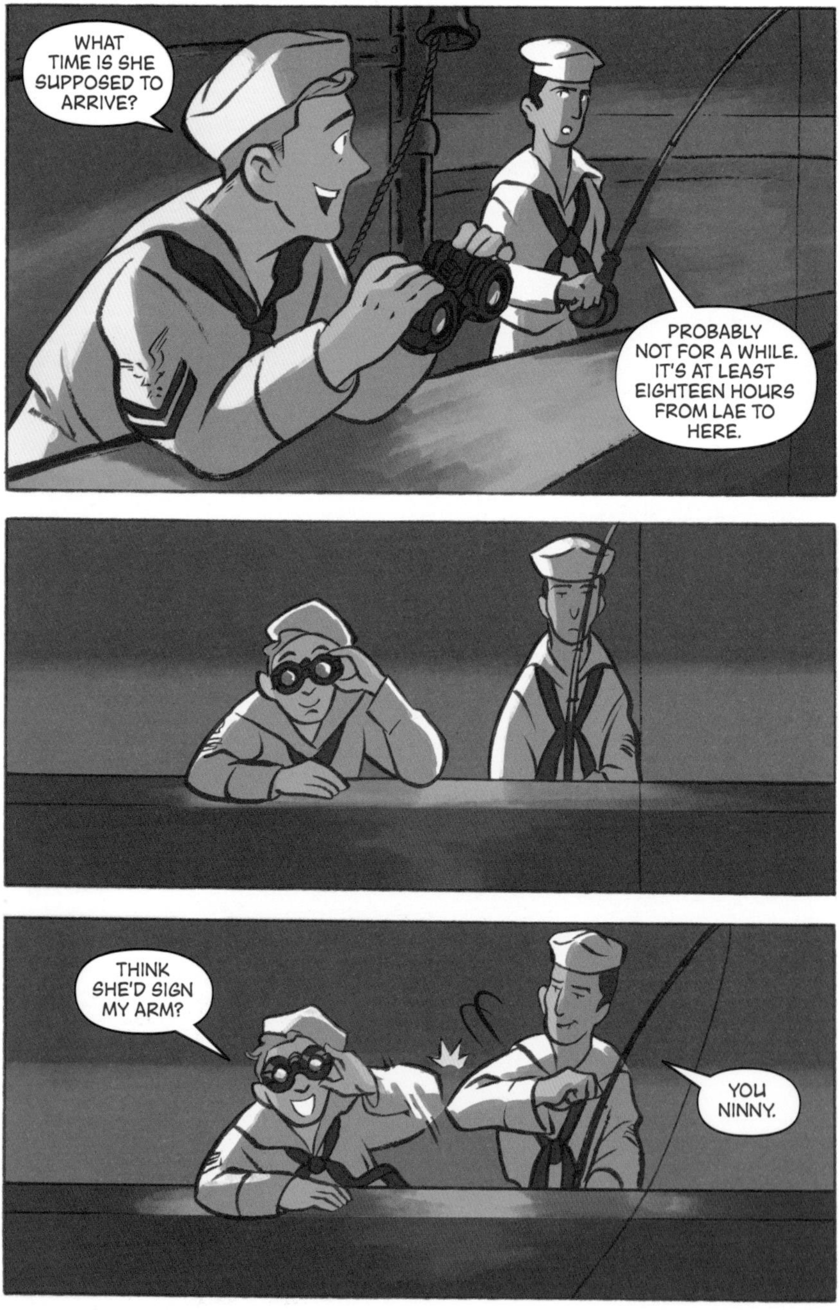
WHAT TIME IS SHE SUPPOSED TO ARRIVE?
PROBABLY NOT FOR A WHILE. IT'S AT LEAST EIGHTEEN HOURS FROM LAE TO HERE.
THINK SHE'D SIGN MY ARM?
YOU NINNY.

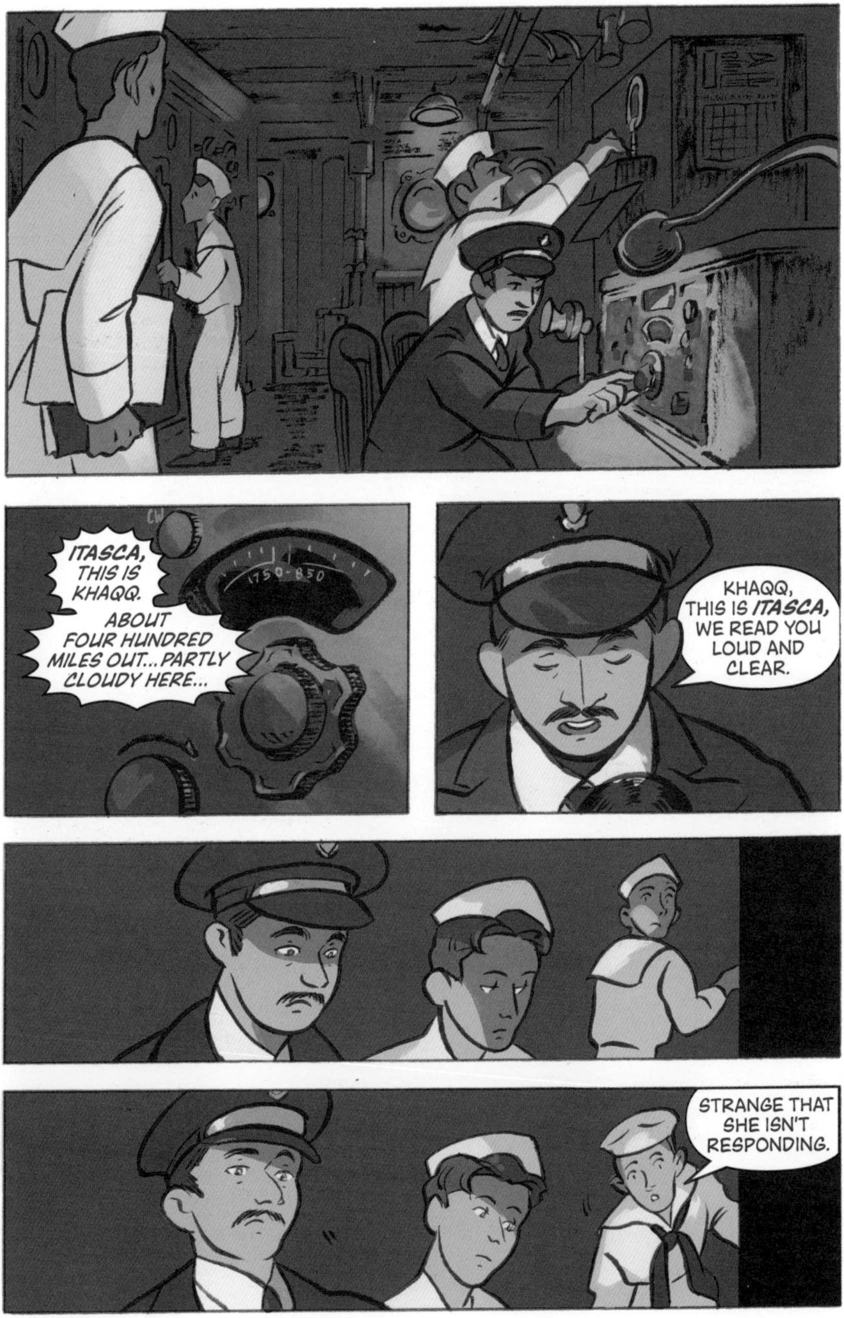
ITASCA, THIS IS KHAQQ.
ABOUT FOUR HUNDRED MILES OUT...PARTLY CLOUDY HERE...
KHAQQ, THIS IS ITASCA, WE READ YOU LOUD AND CLEAR.
STRANGE THAT SHE ISN'T RESPONDING.

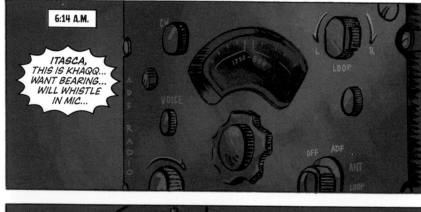

6:14 A.M.

ITASCA, THIS IS KHAQQ... WANT BEARING... WILL WHISTLE IN MIC...

KHAQQ, THIS IS *ITASCA*, WE READ YOU. DO YOU COPY?

TRY TO GET A BEARING ON HER ON THE RADIO DIRECTION FINDER, WILL YOU?

The Radio Direction Finder

Before GPS, many pilots navigated via a radio direction finder (RDF). These direction finders were a loop antenna, which could be turned in a circle to search for signals broadcast by radio stations on certain frequencies. Radio signals would come in strongest when the loop antenna was lined up with them and weakest when the loop antenna was turned 90 degrees away from them. The RDF operator would turn the antenna and listen for the weakest signals (also called a "null"), which were the easiest and most accurate ones to hear. Once they found those "null" signals, they would know the radio station transmitting the beacon was 90 degrees away—and they could point their plane in that direction. Both the Electra and the USCGC *Itasca* had an RDF, with the operator listening on one side of the frequency and the pilot listening on the other.

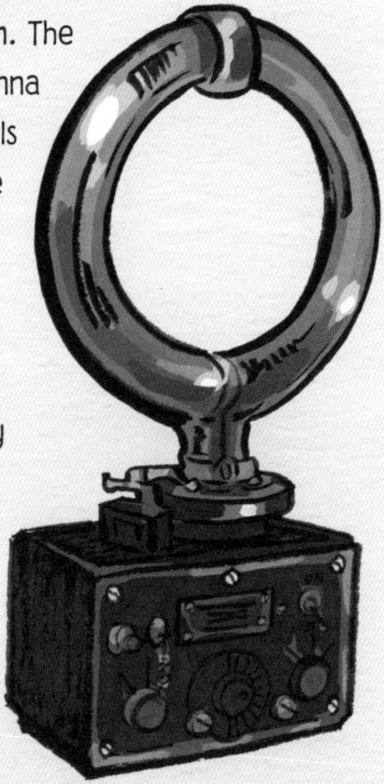

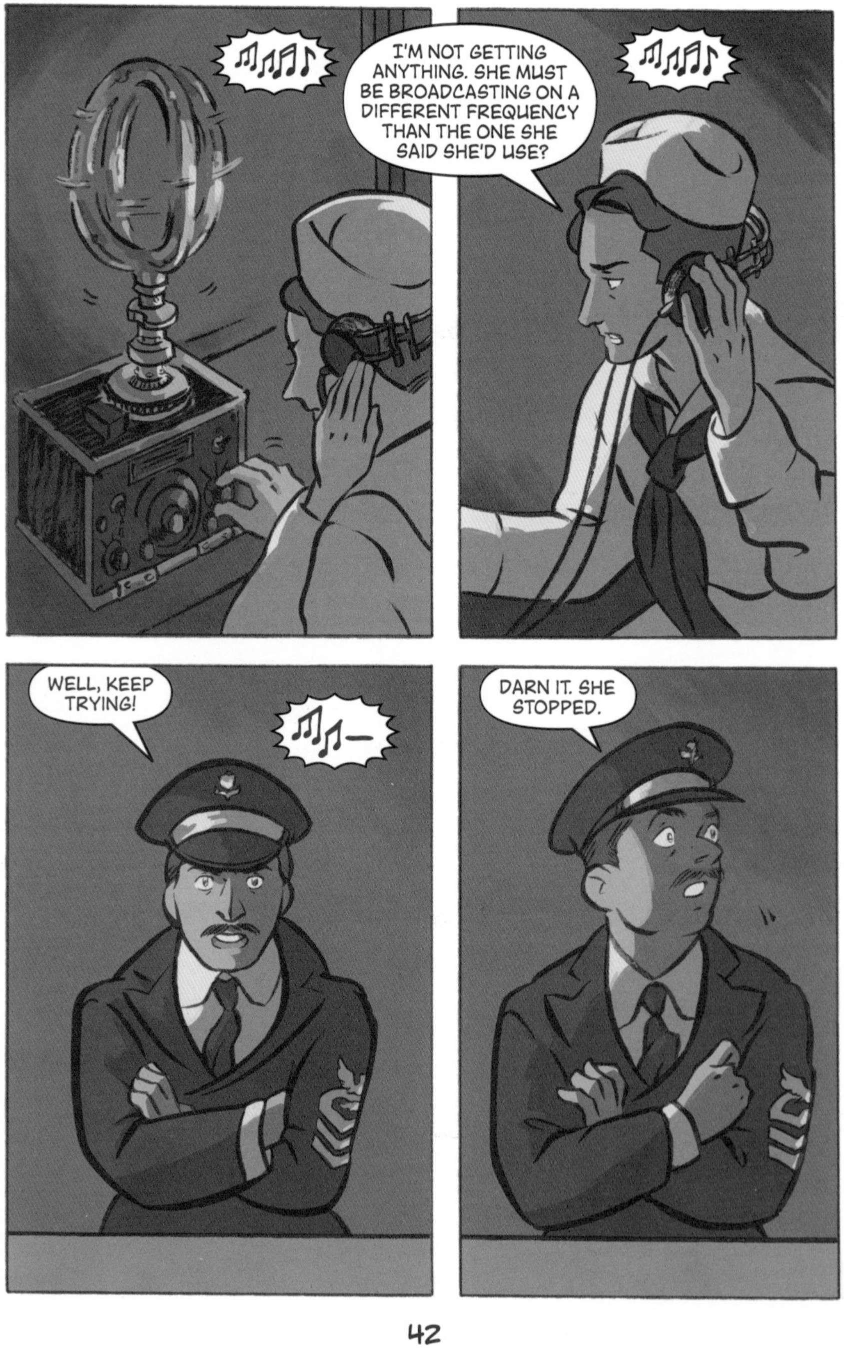
I'M NOT GETTING ANYTHING. SHE MUST BE BROADCASTING ON A DIFFERENT FREQUENCY THAN THE ONE SHE SAID SHE'D USE?
WELL, KEEP TRYING!
DARN IT. SHE STOPPED.

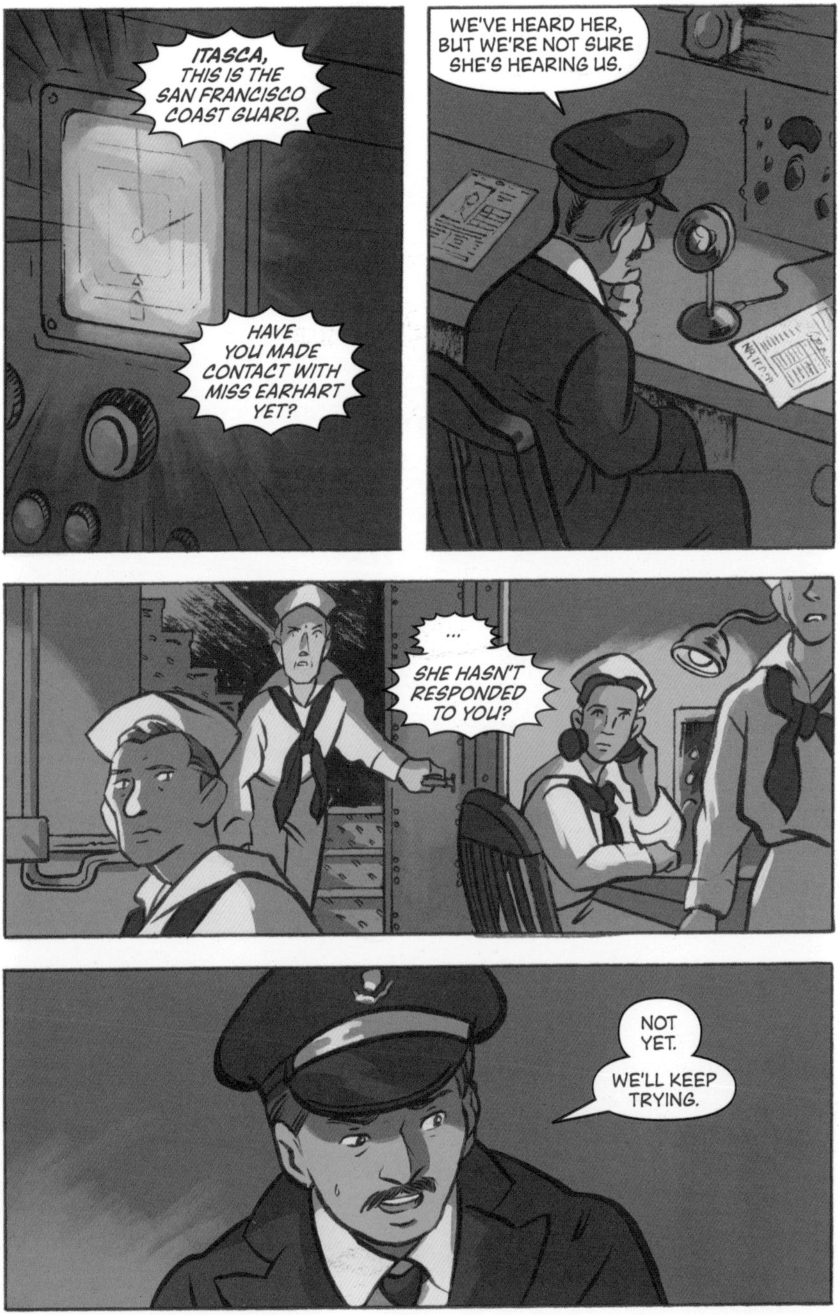
ITASCA, THIS IS THE SAN FRANCISCO COAST GUARD.
HAVE YOU MADE CONTACT WITH MISS EARHART YET?
WE'VE HEARD HER, BUT WE'RE NOT SURE SHE'S HEARING US.
...
SHE HASN'T RESPONDED TO YOU?
NOT YET.
WE'LL KEEP TRYING.

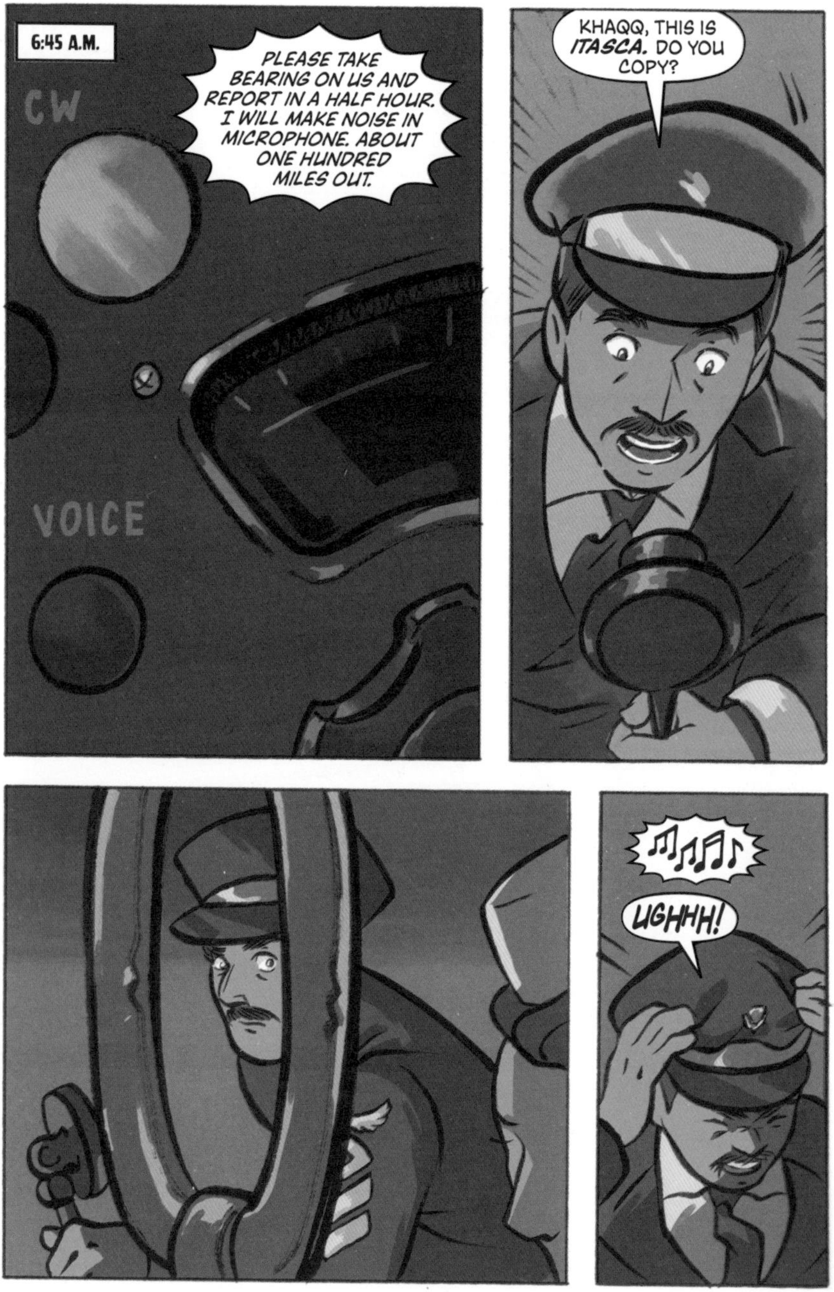
6:45 A.M.
PLEASE TAKE BEARING ON US AND REPORT IN A HALF HOUR. I WILL MAKE NOISE IN MICROPHONE. ABOUT ONE HUNDRED MILES OUT.
CW
VOICE
KHAQQ, THIS IS ITASCA. DO YOU COPY?
♫♫♫♪
UGHHH!

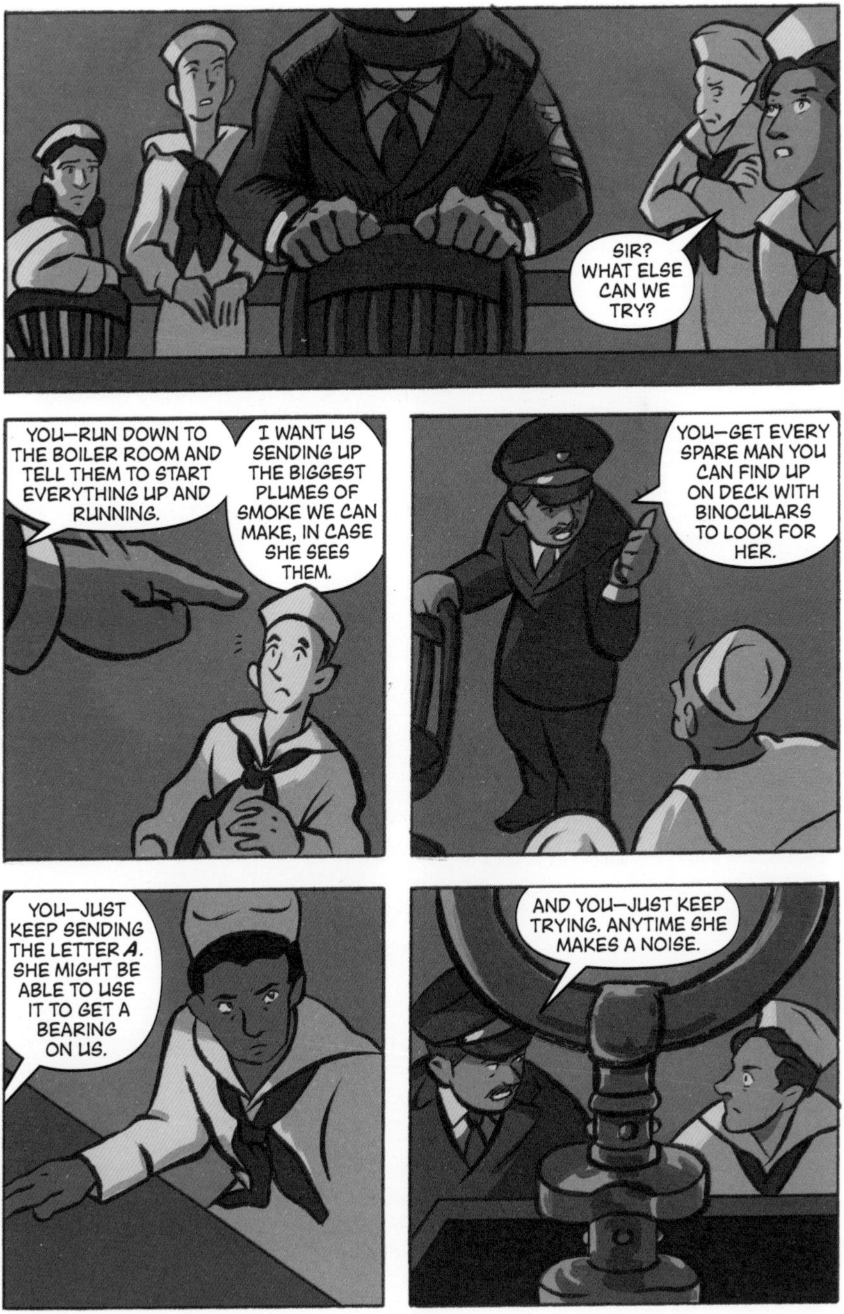
SIR? WHAT ELSE CAN WE TRY?
YOU—RUN DOWN TO THE BOILER ROOM AND TELL THEM TO START EVERYTHING UP AND RUNNING.
I WANT US SENDING UP THE BIGGEST PLUMES OF SMOKE WE CAN MAKE, IN CASE SHE SEES THEM.
YOU—GET EVERY SPARE MAN YOU CAN FIND UP ON DECK WITH BINOCULARS TO LOOK FOR HER.
YOU—JUST KEEP SENDING THE LETTER *A*. SHE MIGHT BE ABLE TO USE IT TO GET A BEARING ON US.
AND YOU—JUST KEEP TRYING. ANYTIME SHE MAKES A NOISE.

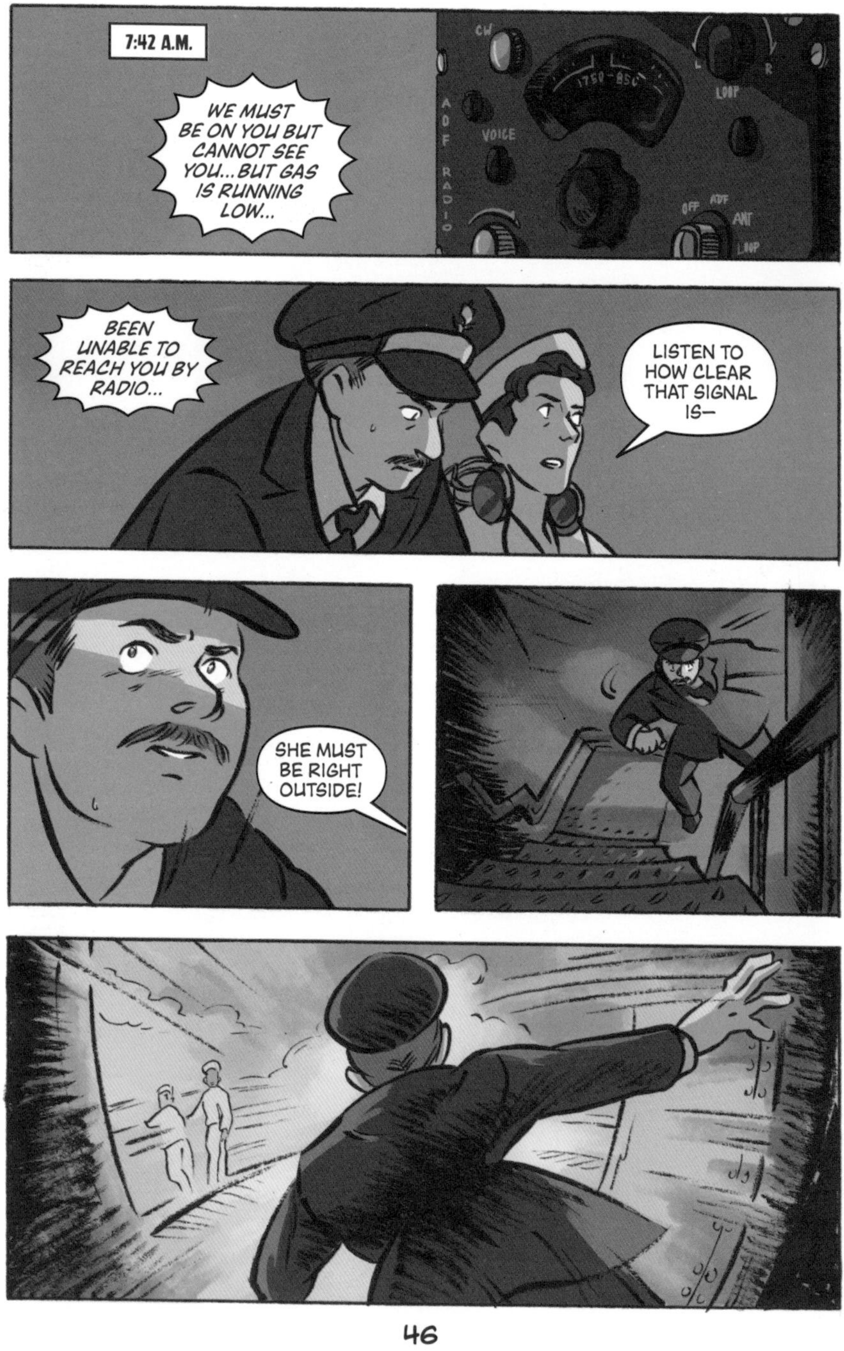
7:42 A.M.
WE MUST BE ON YOU BUT CANNOT SEE YOU... BUT GAS IS RUNNING LOW...
BEEN UNABLE TO REACH YOU BY RADIO...
LISTEN TO HOW CLEAR THAT SIGNAL IS—
SHE MUST BE RIGHT OUTSIDE!

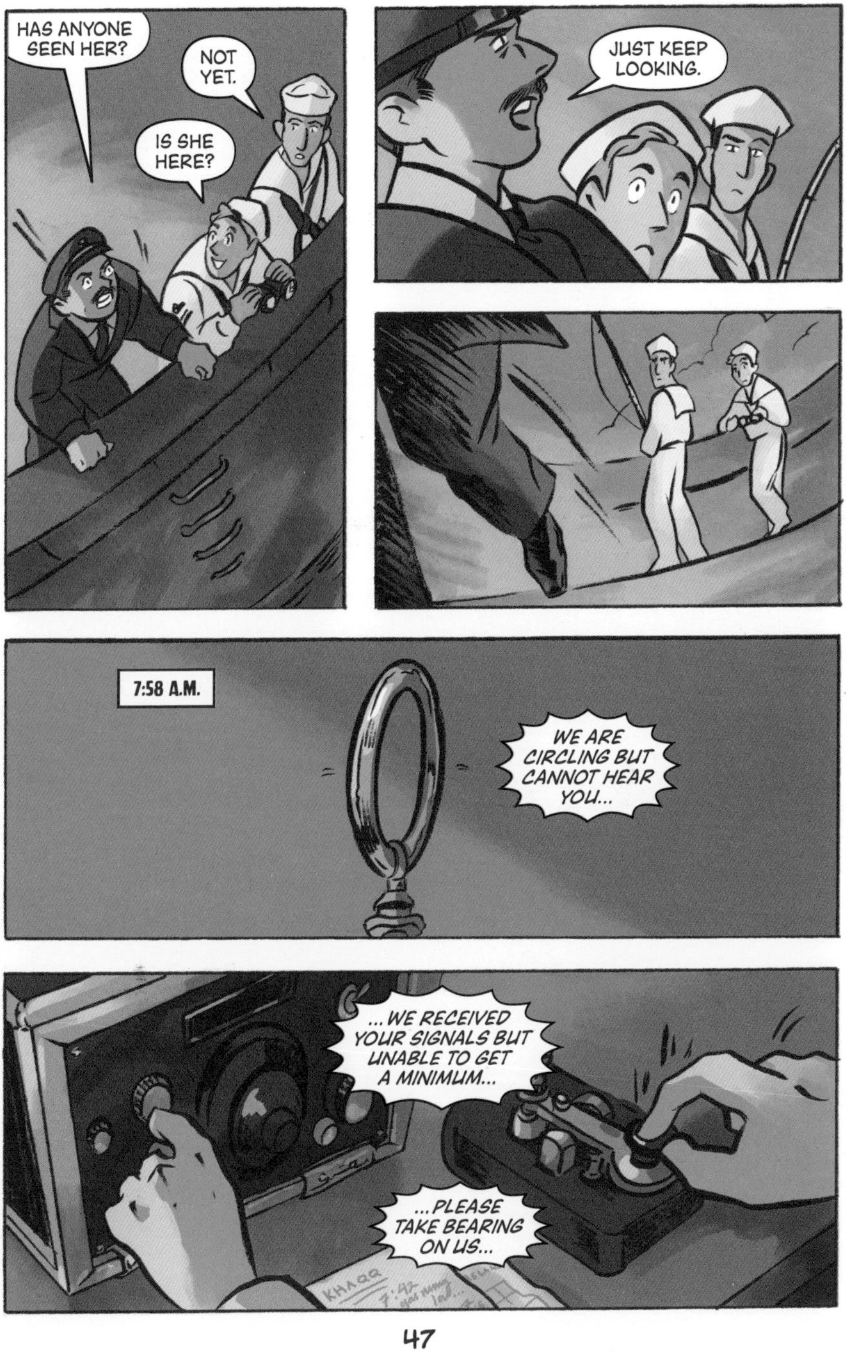
HAS ANYONE SEEN HER?
NOT YET.
IS SHE HERE?
JUST KEEP LOOKING.
7:58 A.M.
WE ARE CIRCLING BUT CANNOT HEAR YOU...
...WE RECEIVED YOUR SIGNALS BUT UNABLE TO GET A MINIMUM...
...PLEASE TAKE BEARING ON US...

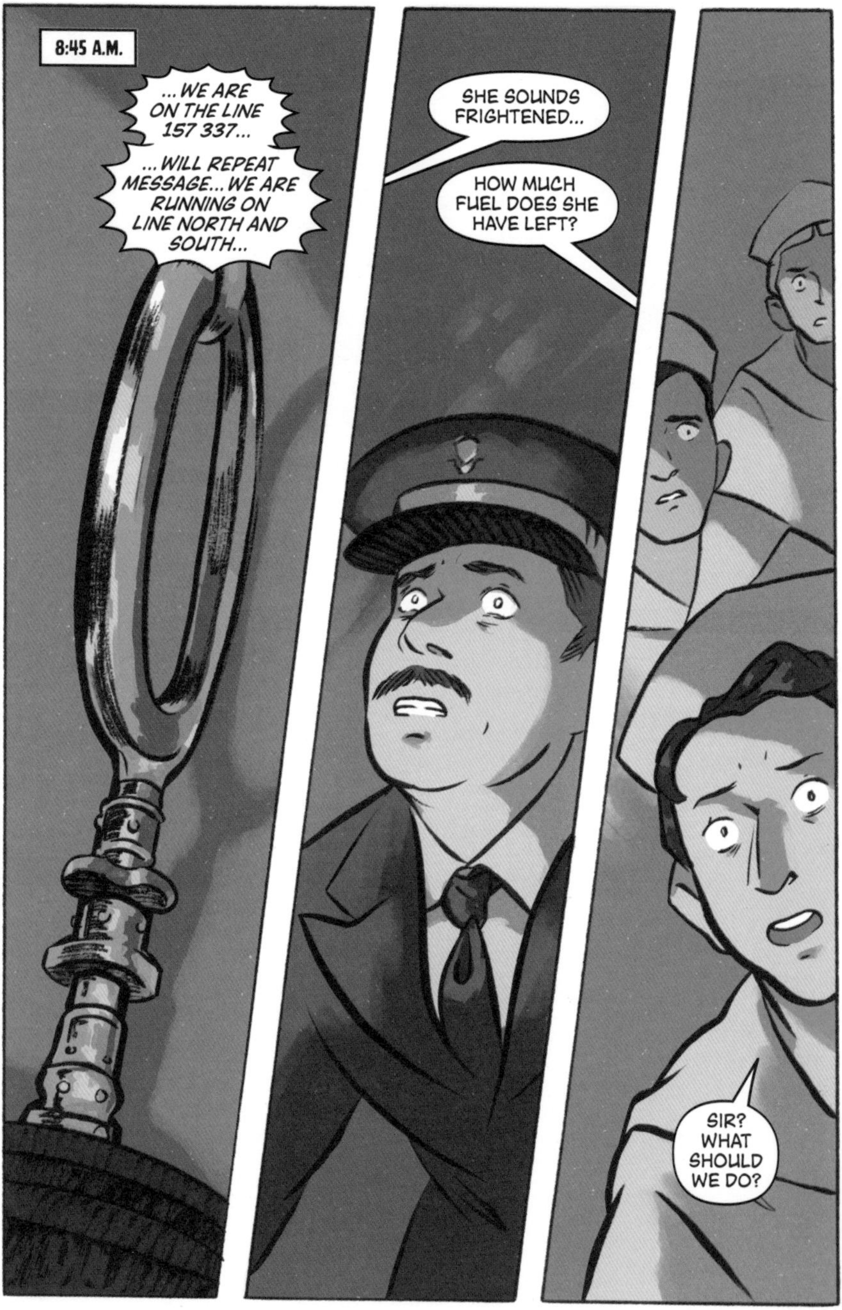
8:45 A.M.
...WE ARE ON THE LINE 157 337...
...WILL REPEAT MESSAGE... WE ARE RUNNING ON LINE NORTH AND SOUTH...
SHE SOUNDS FRIGHTENED...
HOW MUCH FUEL DOES SHE HAVE LEFT?
SIR? WHAT SHOULD WE DO?

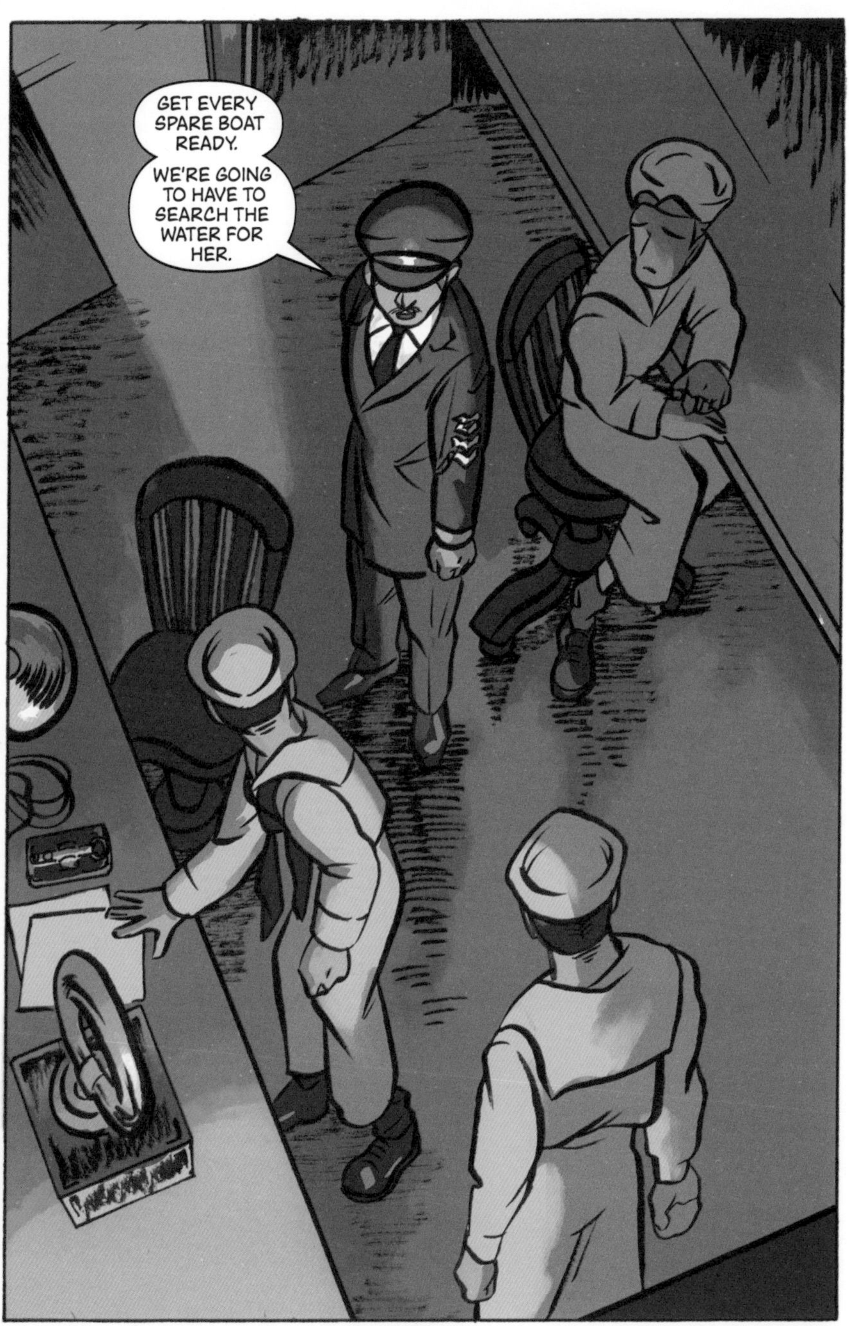
GET EVERY SPARE BOAT READY.
WE'RE GOING TO HAVE TO SEARCH THE WATER FOR HER.

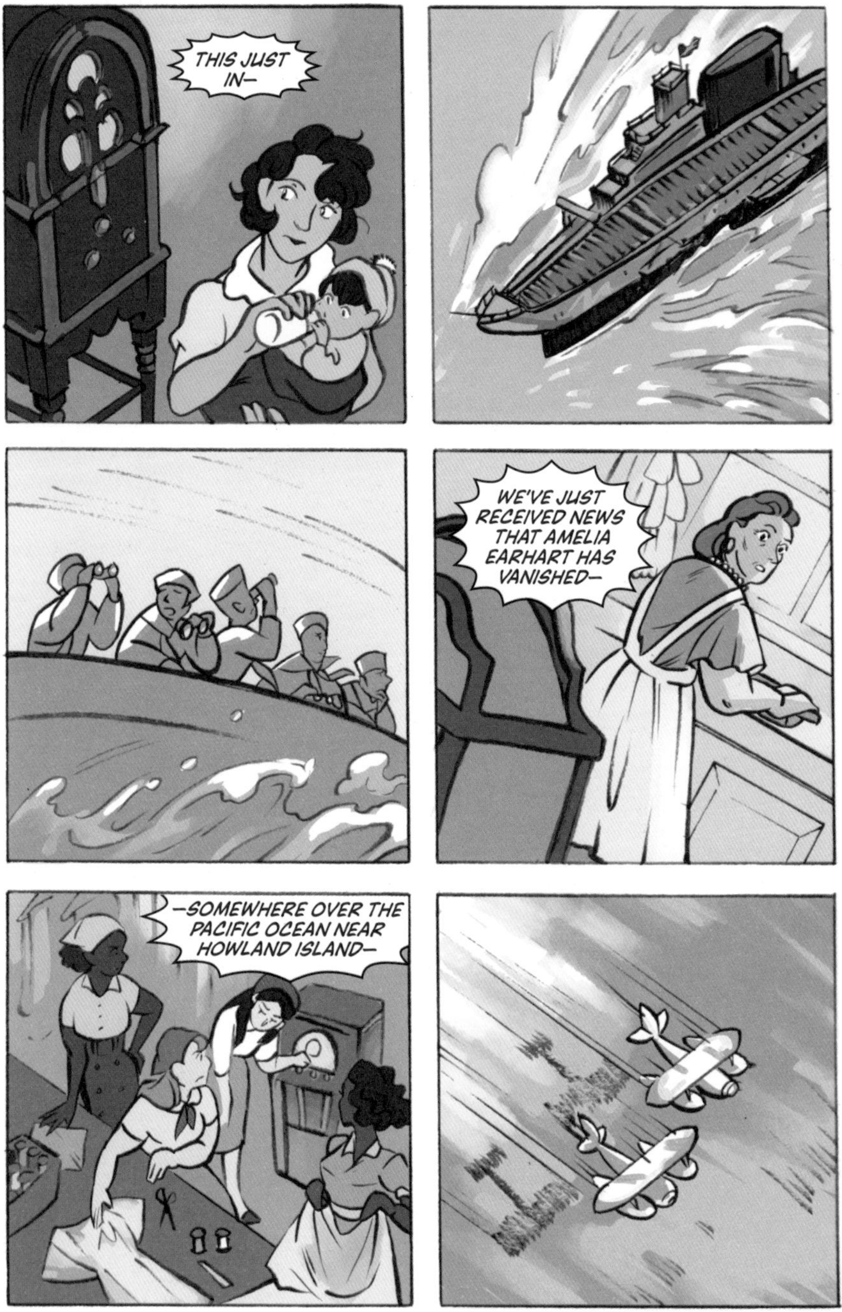
THIS JUST IN—
WE'VE JUST RECEIVED NEWS THAT AMELIA EARHART HAS VANISHED—
—SOMEWHERE OVER THE PACIFIC OCEAN NEAR HOWLAND ISLAND—

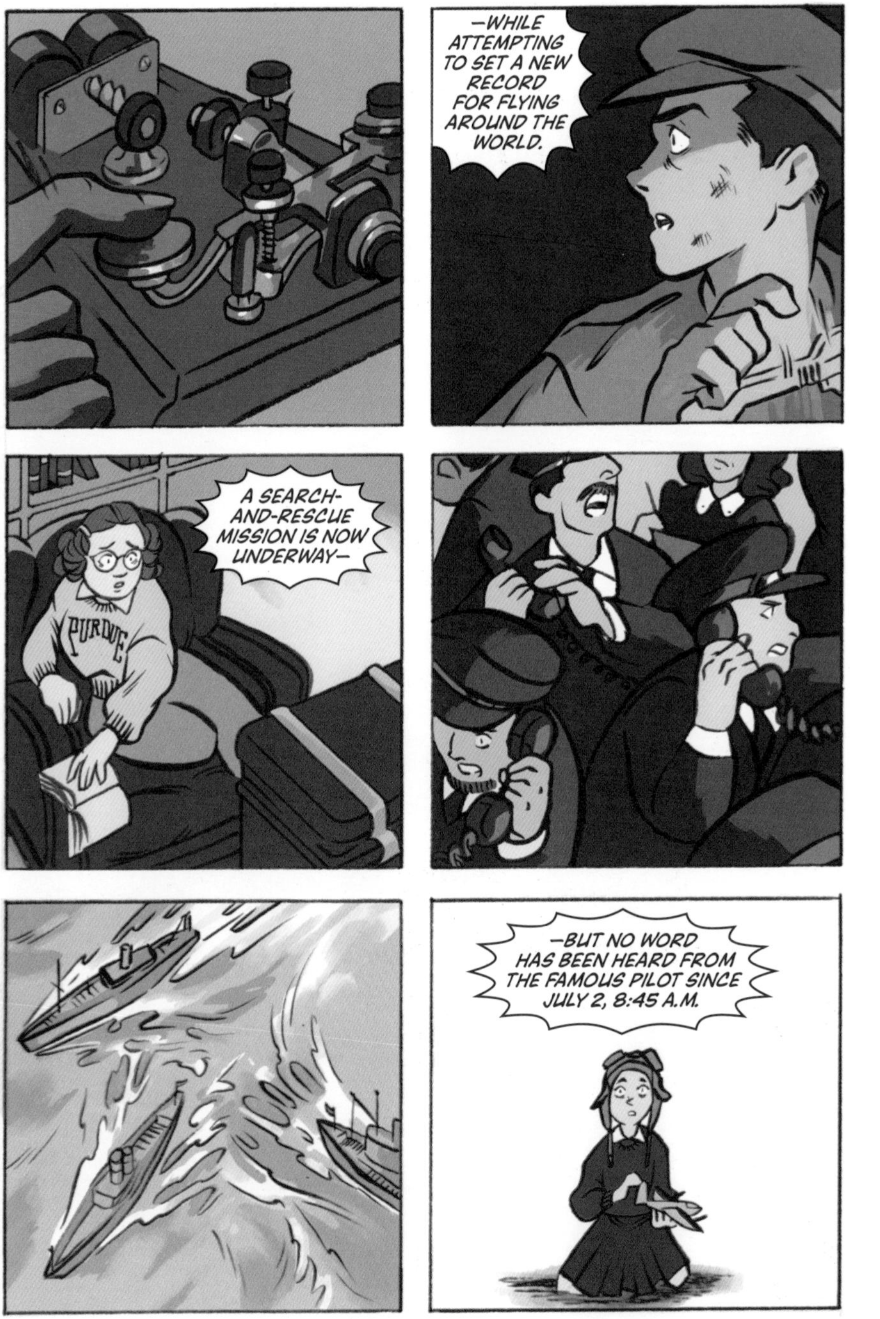
—WHILE ATTEMPTING TO SET A NEW RECORD FOR FLYING AROUND THE WORLD.
A SEARCH-AND-RESCUE MISSION IS NOW UNDERWAY—
PURDUE
—BUT NO WORD HAS BEEN HEARD FROM THE FAMOUS PILOT SINCE JULY 2, 8:45 A.M.

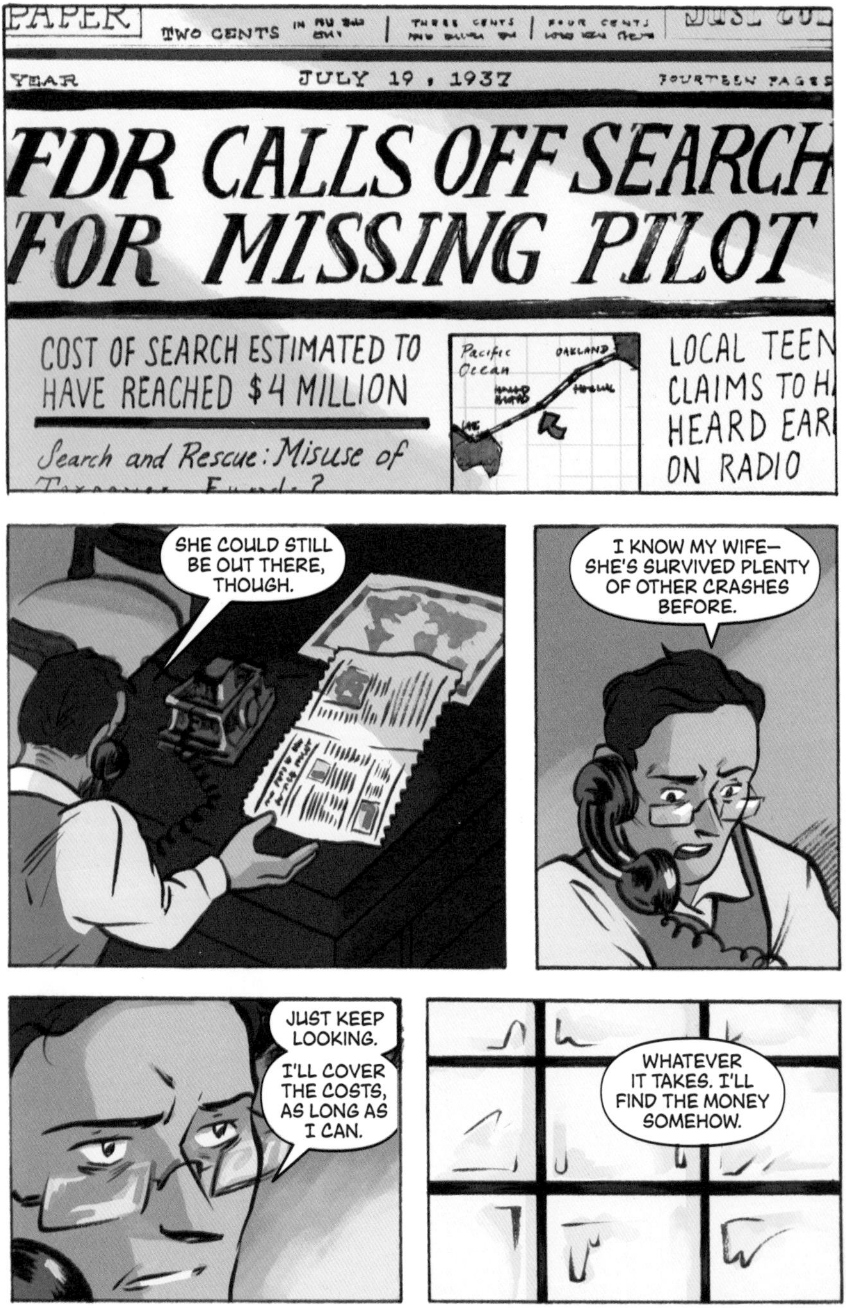

PAPER
TWO CENTS
YEAR
JULY 19, 1937
FDR CALLS OFF SEARCH FOR MISSING PILOT
COST OF SEARCH ESTIMATED TO HAVE REACHED $4 MILLION
Search and Rescue: Misuse of
Pacific Ocean
OAKLAND
LOCAL TEEN
ON RADIO
SHE COULD STILL BE OUT THERE, THOUGH.
I KNOW MY WIFE— SHE'S SURVIVED PLENTY OF OTHER CRASHES BEFORE.
JUST KEEP LOOKING.
I'LL COVER THE COSTS, AS LONG AS I CAN.
WHATEVER IT TAKES. I'LL FIND THE MONEY SOMEHOW.

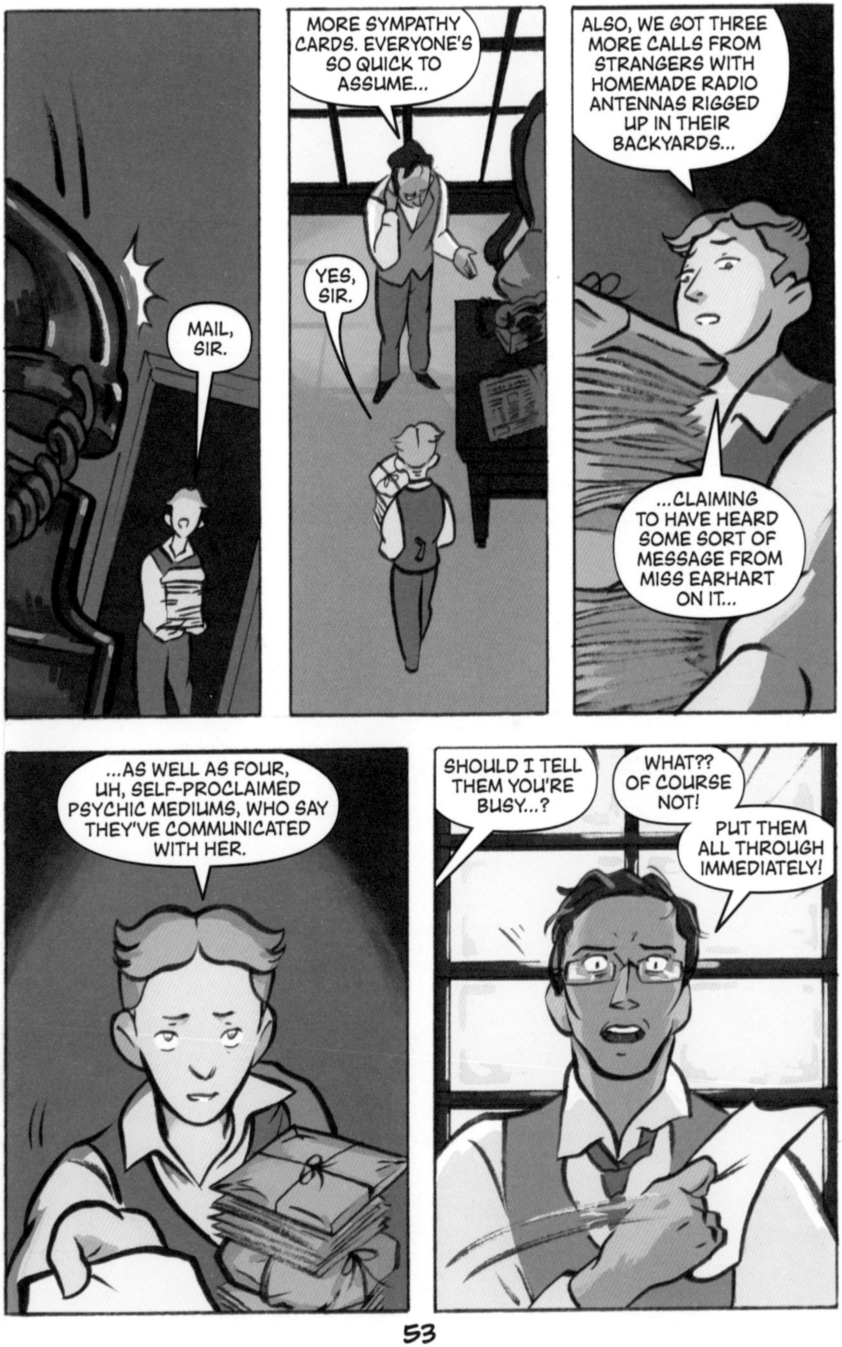
MAIL, SIR.
MORE SYMPATHY CARDS. EVERYONE'S SO QUICK TO ASSUME...
YES, SIR.
ALSO, WE GOT THREE MORE CALLS FROM STRANGERS WITH HOMEMADE RADIO ANTENNAS RIGGED UP IN THEIR BACKYARDS...
...CLAIMING TO HAVE HEARD SOME SORT OF MESSAGE FROM MISS EARHART ON IT...
...AS WELL AS FOUR, UH, SELF-PROCLAIMED PSYCHIC MEDIUMS, WHO SAY THEY'VE COMMUNICATED WITH HER.
SHOULD I TELL THEM YOU'RE BUSY...?
WHAT?? OF COURSE NOT!
PUT THEM ALL THROUGH IMMEDIATELY!

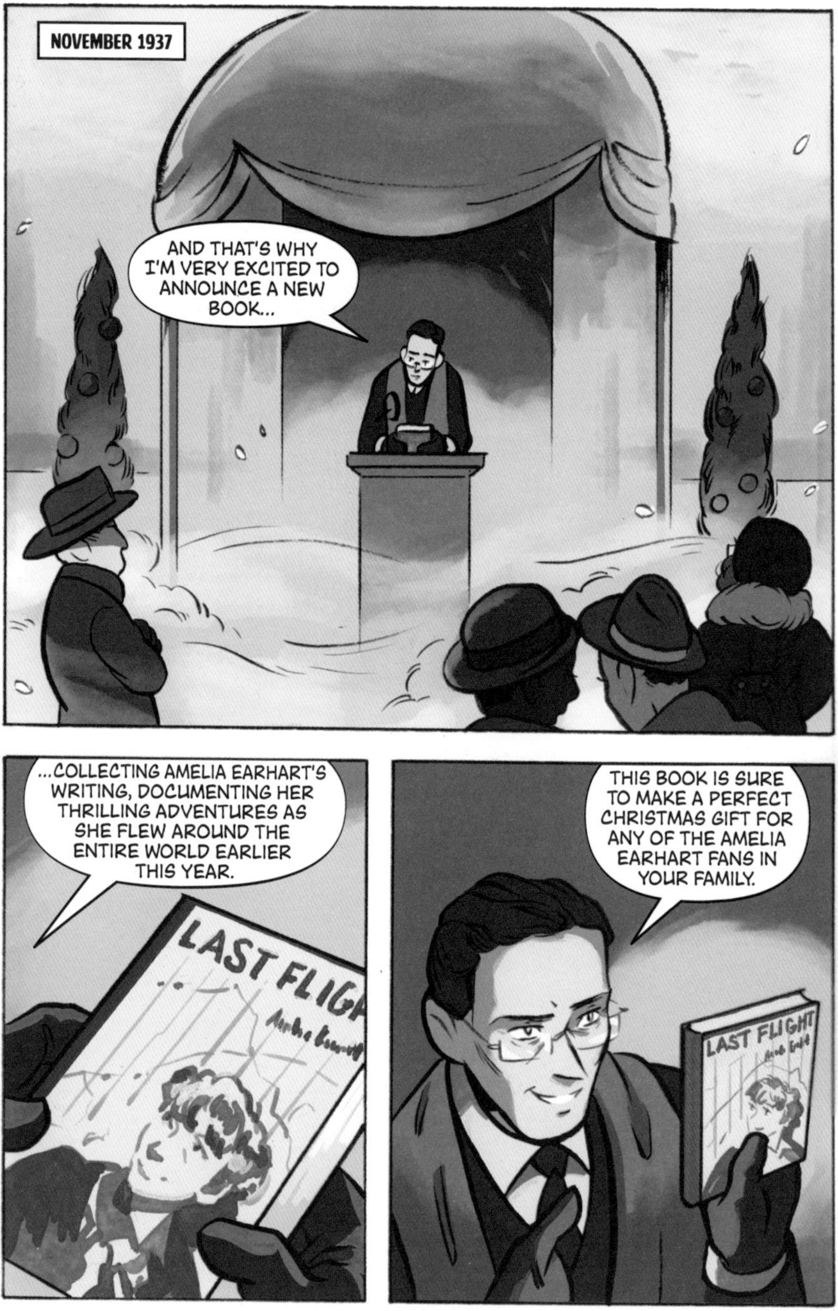
NOVEMBER 1937
AND THAT'S WHY I'M VERY EXCITED TO ANNOUNCE A NEW BOOK...
...COLLECTING AMELIA EARHART'S WRITING, DOCUMENTING HER THRILLING ADVENTURES AS SHE FLEW AROUND THE ENTIRE WORLD EARLIER THIS YEAR.
LAST FLIGH
THIS BOOK IS SURE TO MAKE A PERFECT CHRISTMAS GIFT FOR ANY OF THE AMELIA EARHART FANS IN YOUR FAMILY.
LAST FLIGHT

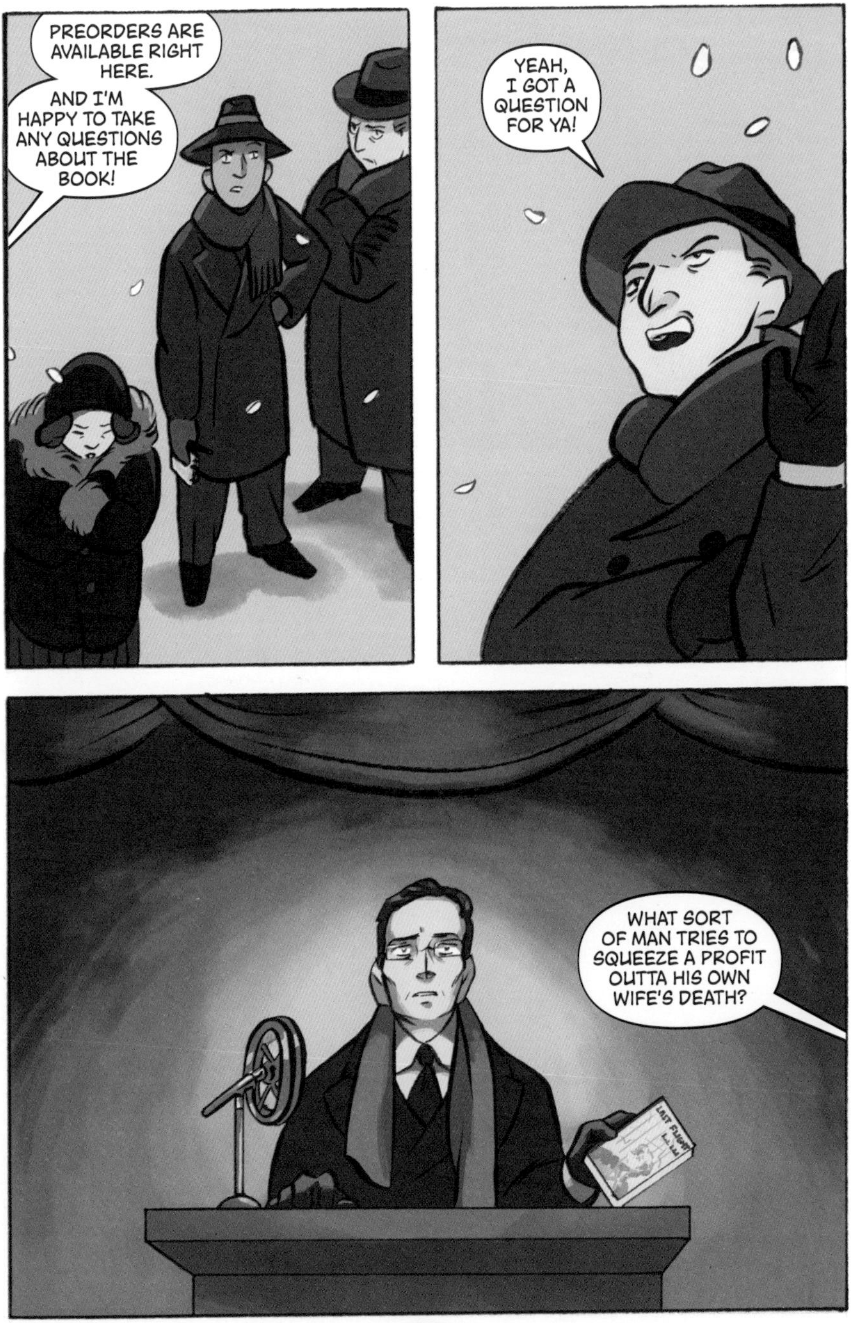
PREORDERS ARE AVAILABLE RIGHT HERE.
AND I'M HAPPY TO TAKE ANY QUESTIONS ABOUT THE BOOK!
YEAH, I GOT A QUESTION FOR YA!
WHAT SORT OF MAN TRIES TO SQUEEZE A PROFIT OUTTA HIS OWN WIFE'S DEATH?

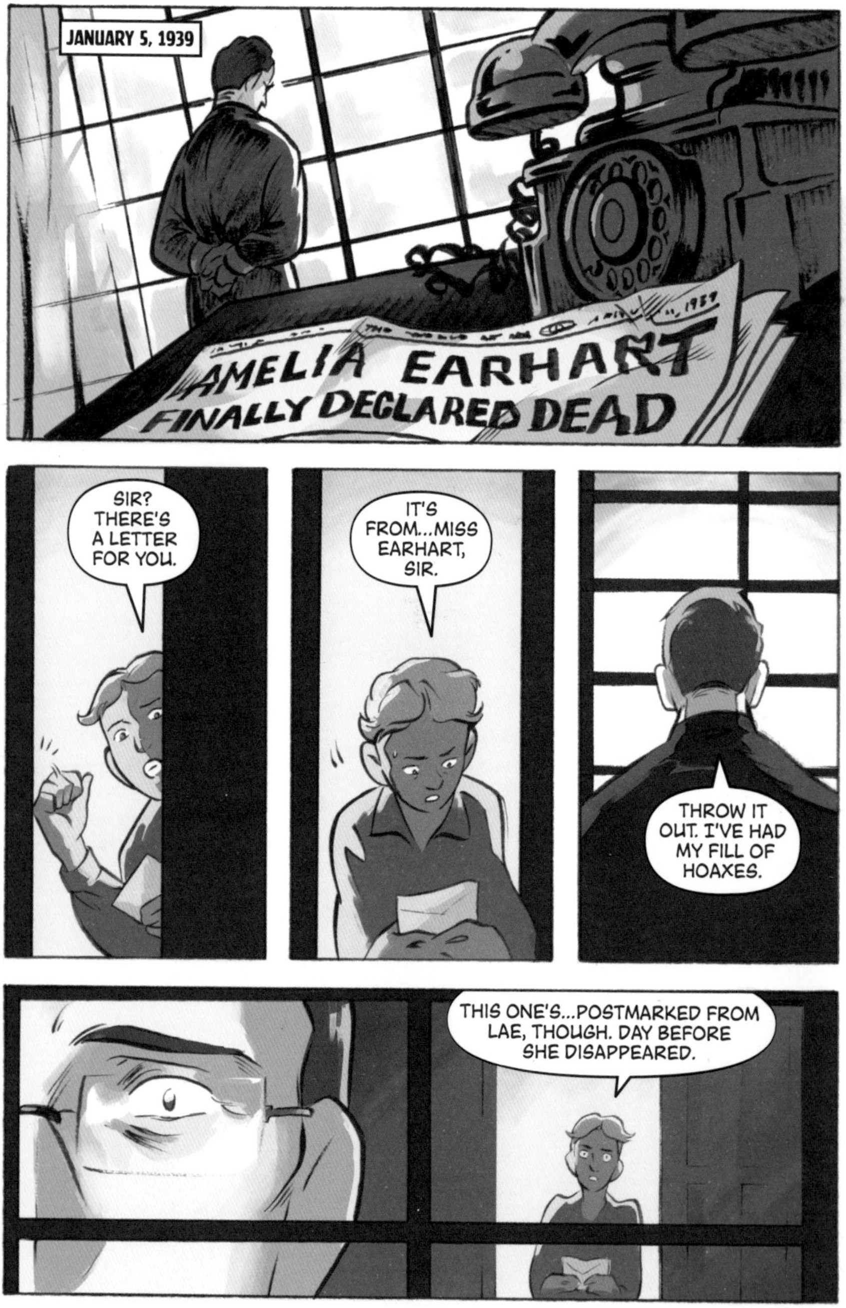
JANUARY 5, 1939
AMELIA EARHART
FINALLY DECLARED DEAD
SIR? THERE'S A LETTER FOR YOU.
IT'S FROM...MISS EARHART, SIR.
THROW IT OUT. I'VE HAD MY FILL OF HOAXES.
THIS ONE'S...POSTMARKED FROM LAE, THOUGH. DAY BEFORE SHE DISAPPEARED.

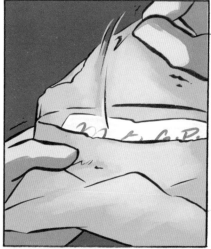

MY DEAR G. P.,

WE HIT SOME STORMY
WEATHER ON THIS LEG
OF OUR JOURNEY—AS
IS BOUND TO HAPPEN
EVENTUALLY ON ANY
LONG-DISTANCE FLIGHT.

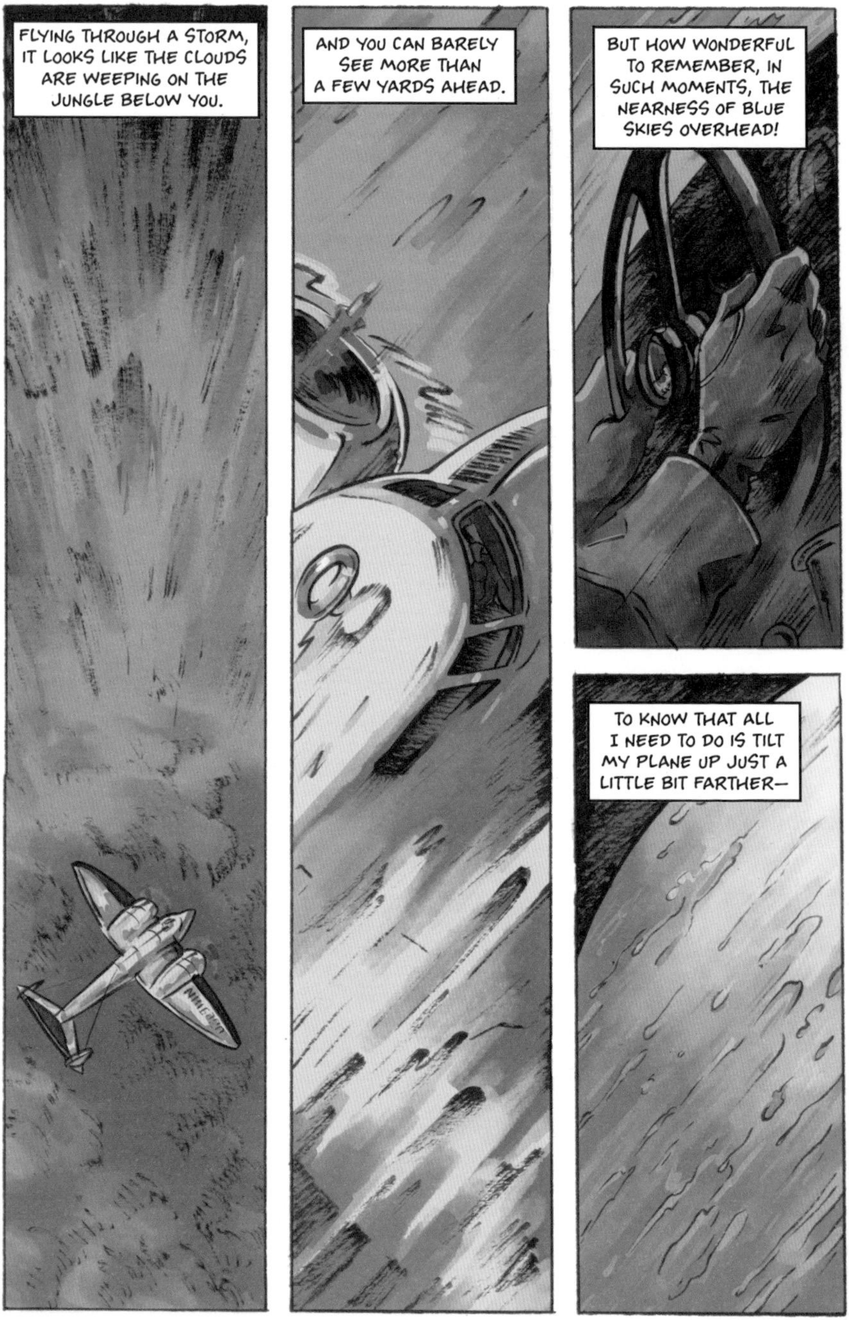
FLYING THROUGH A STORM, IT LOOKS LIKE THE CLOUDS ARE WEEPING ON THE JUNGLE BELOW YOU.
AND YOU CAN BARELY SEE MORE THAN A FEW YARDS AHEAD.
BUT HOW WONDERFUL TO REMEMBER, IN SUCH MOMENTS, THE NEARNESS OF BLUE SKIES OVERHEAD!
TO KNOW THAT ALL I NEED TO DO IS TILT MY PLANE UP JUST A LITTLE BIT FARTHER—

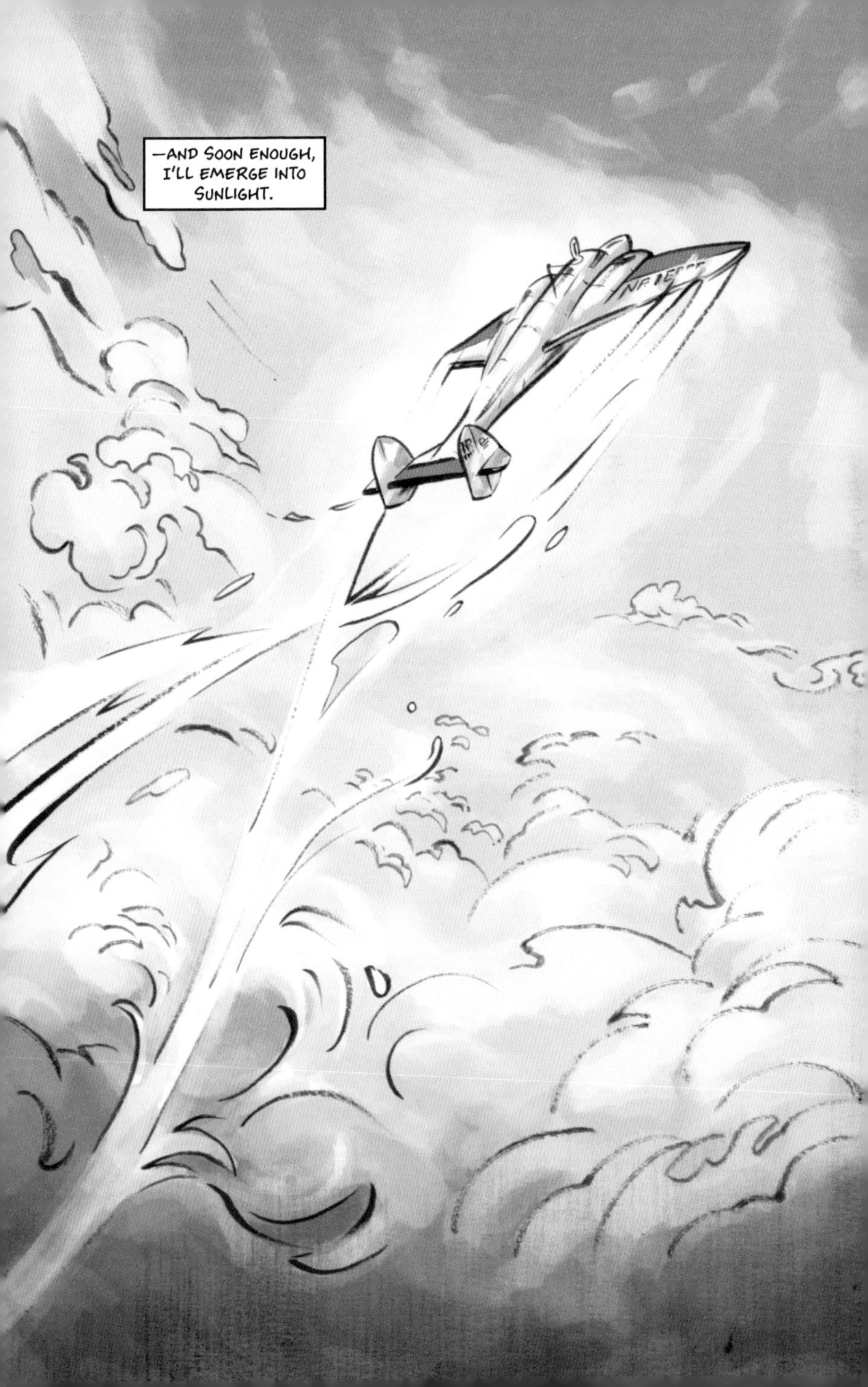
—AND SOON ENOUGH, I'LL EMERGE INTO SUNLIGHT.

Conclusion

Many theories have been proposed that try to explain what happened to Amelia. Some people think she crashed her plane on a different island and possibly lived there for a short while—though no conclusive evidence of this has been found. Some people believe she may have been captured by the Japanese military and taken prisoner—but this belief was most likely a result of rising tensions between the United States and Japan in the years leading up to World War II. In fact, Japan helped the United States search for Amelia after her disappearance. In 1970, an author named Joe Klaas wrote a book claiming that Amelia Earhart was living in New Jersey under the pseudonym Irene Bolam—but this was quickly disputed by Irene Bolam herself, who certainly was not Amelia Earhart.

Many historians believe Amelia ran out of fuel while looking for Howland Island, and her plane crashed somewhere in the Pacific Ocean. The plane has not been found because it would have sunk—and it's not easy to find a very small plane in the middle of a very large and very deep ocean. Many other planes and ships have been lost the same way, all throughout history.

Amelia's story, and the tragedy of her final trip around the world, has captured people's imaginations for nearly a century. Her life has been immortalized in dozens of books, movies, and

documentaries. Amelia also has another legacy that has left a major mark on American history: the way she inspired women to go after jobs in science and engineering, fields previously considered "men's work." Amelia fought to prove that women were equal to men in the air; soon after her death, during World War II, thousands of other women would take up that same fight in their chosen industries.

Amelia's life is proof that our actions can inspire others. When we fight for equality, we can show people around us what is possible and help build a better world.

U·S· AIR MAIL
8¢
AMELIA EARHART

Timeline of Amelia Earhart's Life

1897 — Amelia Earhart is born in Atchison, Kansas

1921 — Begins taking flying lessons

1928 — Becomes the first woman to fly across the Atlantic as a passenger

1931 — Marries G. P. Putnam

1932 — Becomes the first woman to fly solo across the Atlantic

1935 — Becomes the first person to fly solo across the Pacific

1936 — Purdue agrees to buy her the Lockheed 10-E Electra, later nicknamed the "flying laboratory"

1937 — Unsuccessfully attempts first around-the-world trip with Fred Noonan, Harry Manning, and Paul Mantz in March from Oakland, California.

— Embarks on her second attempt at an around-the-world flight from Miami, Florida, in July, accompanied only by Fred Noonan

— Plane disappears near Howland Island

— US government searches for Amelia and Fred

— President Roosevelt calls off the search; G. P. will continue financing a smaller search himself

— In October, having exhausted his own financial resources, G. P. calls off his search for his wife

1939 — A court in Los Angeles declares Amelia legally dead

Bibliography

*Books for young readers

Butler, Susan. *East to the Dawn: The Life of Amelia Earhart*. New York: Da Capo Press, 1999.

*Doak, Robin S. *Amelia Earhart*. Chicago: Heinemann Library, 2013.

Earhart, Amelia. *Last Flight*. New York: Harcourt, Brace and Company, 1937.

Expedition Amelia. Produced by National Geographic, 2019. TV documentary film.

*Fleming, Candace. *Amelia Lost: The Life and Disappearance of Amelia Earhart*. New York: Schwarz & Wade, 2011.

Negroni, Christine. *The Crash Detectives: Investigating the World's Most Mysterious Air Disasters*. New York: Penguin Books, 2016.

O'Brien, Keith. *Fly Girls: How Five Daring Women Defied All Odds and Made Aviation History*. Boston: Houghton Mifflin Harcourt, 2018.

Porter, Nancy, dir. *Amelia Earhart: The Price of Courage*. Produced by WGBH, 1993. PBS American Experience documentary film.

Thurman, Judith. "Amelia Earhart's Last Flight." *New Yorker*, September 14, 2009. https://www.newyorker.com/magazine/2009/09/14/missing-woman.

Website

collections.lib.purdue.edu/aearhart (Purdue Libraries' Amelia Earhart Collection)

ABOUT THE CREATORS

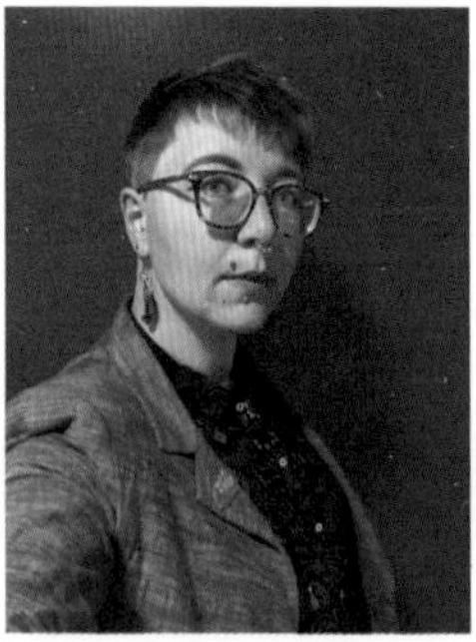

Melanie Gillman is a cartoonist who specializes in LGBTQ books for kids and teens. They are the creator of the webcomic and graphic novel *As the Crow Flies*, published in 2017 by Iron Circus Comics, and winner of the 2018 Stonewall Honor Award. They are also the author of *Stage Dreams*, published by Lerner/ Graphic Universe in 2019. In addition to their graphic novel work, they are also a senior lecturer in the Comics MFA program at the California College of the Arts.

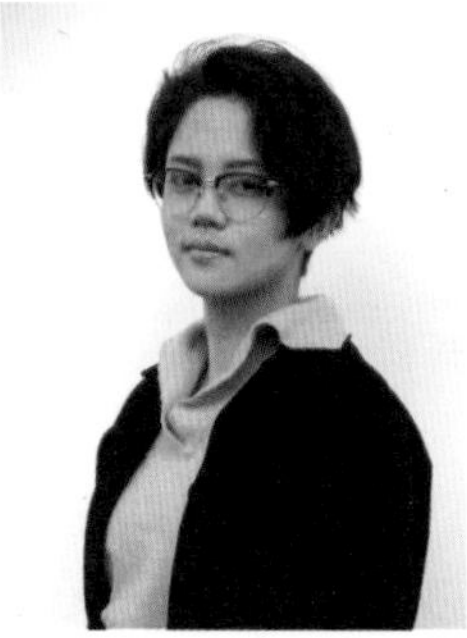

A.C. Esguerra is an award-winning comics author and artist who draws mainly with traditional ink. They were the creator of *Eighty Days*, a queer historical romance about 1930s pilots, published by Archaia in 2021. They have illustrated for BOOM! Studios (*Adventure Time*) and the San Francisco Arts Commission (*Art on Market Street Kiosk Poster Series*), among others. They are a Visiting Author for Lambda Literary's LGBTQ+ Writers in Schools Program and have exhibited their art in galleries internationally. Born in Manila, Philippines, they now live in Los Angeles with their partner and a very good Shiba Inu.